ESCHATOLOGY: THE SIGNS OF THE TIMES OF JESUS CHRIST'S SOON RETURN

HIS COMING IS CLOSER THAN YOU THINK

REV. SANDRA Y. WASHINGTON

BLACKCURRANT PRESS
New York

ESCHATOLOGY: THE SIGNS OF THE TIMES OF
JESUS CHRIST'S SOON RETURN
HIS COMING IS CLOSER THAN YOU THINK

Revised Edition Printed By Blackcurrant Press. Books may be ordered
through booksellers or by contacting: www.blackcurrantpress.com

Because of the dynamic nature of the Internet, any Web addresses or links
contained in this book may have changed since publication and may no
longer be valid. The views expressed in this work are solely those of the
author and do not necessarily reflect the views of the publisher, and the
publisher hereby disclaims any responsibility for them.

ISBN: 978-1-4401-8407-9 (sc)
ISBN: 978-1-4401-8408-6 (ebk)
ISBN: 978-0-9903-7810-5

Printed in the United States of America

iUniverse rev. date: 11/19/2009

Blackcurrant Press rev. date 05/10/2014

DEDICATION

This book is dedicated to God, the Father, God, the Son, Jesus Christ and God, the Holy Spirit - my Comforter, Helper and Friend for inspiring me to write my thesis on "Eschatology: Signs Of The Times Of Jesus Christ's Soon Return" and publish it as a book. The topic was chosen to do for a research thesis which was one of the requirements to complete the Masters Degree correspondent program in theology sponsored by the Christian International School of Theology in Santa Rosa Beach, FL. The thesis was approved by C.I.S.T. advisors.

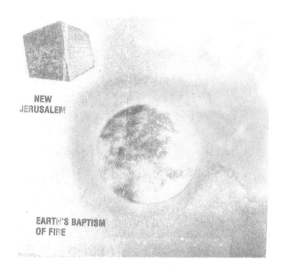

NEW
JERUSALEM

EARTH'S BAPTISM
OF FIRE

Those who read this book shall be blessed and will be prepared with information concerning the signs of the times of Jesus Christ's imminent coming. You can be ready to be a candidate for Christ to rapture you when you accept Christ in your life. Jesus Christ will provide for you to live with Him and His Father in the City of New Jerusalem during the Perfect Age or the Age of Eternity after the Millennial Age. There will be a New Earth and a New Heaven after they are renovated by fire.

ACKNOWLEDGMENTS

Many thanks to all of the teachers of Eschatology such as, Dr. Hilton Sutton, Dr. Jack Van Impe, Leon Bates, Dr. Charles Blair, Pastor John Hagee, Prof. Hal Lindsey and many others listed in the bibliography whose materials have inspired me and given me sound information concerning the signs of the times of the coming Messiah, Jesus Christ. They have given me more understanding interpreting highlights of the Book of Revelation as well.

Many thanks to Rev. Pastor Michael Gissentanna and his wife, Min. Doreen Gissentanna for their encouragement for me to teach the highlights of the Book of Revelation and the Signs of the Times of Jesus Christ's Soon Return to their congregation at The First Calvary Baptist Church in Inwood, N.Y. I thank them for their faith in me and support. This experience inspired me to teach the subject again at the Jamaica Hospital Chapel to interested medical staff members in Jamaica, Queens, N.Y.

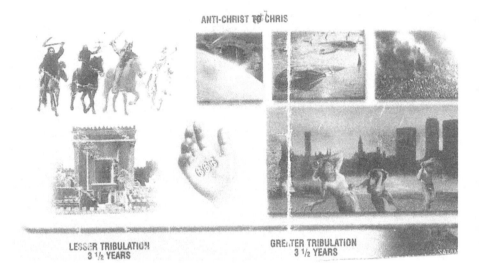

ANTI-CHRIST TO CHRIS

LESSER TRIBULATION
3 ½ YEARS

GREATER TRIBULATION
3 ½ YEARS

Now is the time to receive salvation before the Rapture event. You don't want to be left behind to experience the seven year Great Tribulation on earth. Only Jesus Christ can deliver you from the Great Tribulation if you choose Him as your Savior. If you call upon His Name you shall be saved. **Romans 10:13**

COMPLIMENTS

In January, 2008, Rev. Washington taught an Eschatology class at the First Calvary Baptist Church. The class was clarifying, informative and impactful. She was able to efficiently work through the Book of Revelation within her time constraints. Rev. Washington has proven her eschatological knowledge and her ability to communicate that knowledge to others.

By Rev. Michael J. Gissentanna

Rev. Washington, thank you very much for teaching the medical staff friends and myself about Eschatology. Although Eschatology is not so easy to understand, I now have a better understanding of it after reading the notes several times. I have finally realized how much God truly loves the Church Body of Christ when He provides a way of escape from the Great Tribulation by way of the Rapture. Those who have not accepted Christ will not be prepared for the Rapture and will have to suffer through the Great Tribulation. However, if they do accept Christ, they will have a second chance. I hope to be caught up in the Rapture. I am making myself ready with the help of the Holy Spirit. May God continue to bless you!

By Mrs. Iona Emsley, student

Rev. Washington is a teacher of the gospel who teaches with love and passion; especially when she taught the class on Signs of the Times and the highlights of the Book of Revelation. She was determined to make sure that the people who attended her class, came to the knowledge of God's existence as she described the validity of scriptural prophecies that have manifested and is still manifesting. I thank Rev. Washington for being my teacher for the past year at the Jamaica Hospital where I work.

By Regine Jean-Pierre

I want to thank Rev. Sandra Washington for helping me to understand God's Word. The class on Eschatology she taught at Jamaica Hospital Chapel awoke my mind, faith and soul to the realization of how important we all are to God when He prepares us for the coming of Jesus Christ with the knowledge of prophetic signs occurring in our lifetime. His coming is closer than I thought.

By Vianne Santos

Contents

INTRODUCTION

Eschatology is a term used in Christian theology to be the study of end-time events that began at the beginning of the Church Age to the end of the seven year period of the Great Tribulation, which will usher in the second coming of Jesus Christ to set up His Millennial Reign on the earth. The definition of Eschatology will be discussed further in this section of the book.

This book is mainly written to proclaim the signs of the times of Jesus Christ's coming. The signs of the times describe those events that tell us we're living in the last days of Jesus Christ's soon return, to secretly "catch away" those people who have accepted Him in their lives, before that great and terrible day of God's Wrath called the Great Tribulation. As one hears on the news media, terrifying events are intensifying, and as they intensify, it's a signal to the readers of this book to prepare themselves for the soon arrival of Jesus' coming. No one knows the day nor the hour of His coming, however, one can sense intuitively, or with their spiritual senses, that we are living in the last days of the Church Age. These last days signal Jesus Christ's close return for His body of church members who have His resurrection Spirit, called His Holy Spirit. This will be discussed more as you read on further. The meaning of rapture or the catching away will also be discussed in Chapter 3.

There seems to be some misunderstanding about whether or not there will be a catching away of the body of Christ, and if there is a catching away by Christ, there is confusion as to when it will occur. There are some theologians who believe that Christians are suffering in a Great Tribulation today because of the wickedness in the world, and that the catching away (or the rapture) can occur during the mid or post-tribulation.

As a result of this belief, some Christians and theologians are either unaware or take for granted the signs of the times prophesied in the scriptures that lead to the coming of Jesus Christ to rapture His Church, the body of Christ.

There seems to be some misunderstanding about the occurrence of the Millennial reign of Jesus Christ. Some theologians teach that there will be no pre-millennial reign of Christ, because it already exists spiritually in the hearts of each Christian and that eventually, through evangelism, the world will come to know Jesus and be at peace. Thus, there is no need for Jesus to set up His Millennial reign at His second coming on earth, because His Millennial reign would already be existing before His second coming.

It is for the reason above that the author felt a need to clarify, correct, and comfort those Christians and theologians who have such misunderstandings mentioned concerning the signs of the times which will lead to the close return of Jesus Christ to rapture the body of Christ and its occurrence. The author will discuss the occurrence of God's wrath upon the wicked only, called the Great Tribulation, the occurrence of the Millennial Age and Perfect Age through the use of scriptures and the use of other resource materials to verify her proof on these issues mentioned above.

The author's purposes for her subject title are as follows:

- To stress how important it is to be aware of the signs of the times of events that tell we are living in the end-times for Christ's close return for the Body of Christ.
- To define and discuss the occurrence of the Rapture and what will take place.
- To prove that the Rapture is a Pre-tribulation event vs. the Mid-tribulation and Post-tribulation events.
- To prove that there will be a Pre-Millennium Reign of Christ vs. Amillennium and Post-Millennium Reigns.

Background leading to selection of subject: The author is addressing the subject of this thesis to her fellow believers of the body of Christ which includes the ministers of the five-fold ministry. It would be good information for the unbelievers as well. The author is inspired to proclaim about the Signs of the Times of Jesus Christ's Soon Return to alert the body of Christ as well as the unbeliever to be prepared spiritually, living holy lives. Why? Many unbelievers and even those in the body of Christ do not realize how close the return of Jesus Christ really is. The author notices that most members of the body of Christ are complacent of the events that are happening right before their eyes that tell that Jesus' coming for the church body is imminent. The unbelievers do not know at all. It is hoped that the reading of this book will be a wake-up call to remind the complacent Christians and alert the unbelievers through evangelism, to the latest signs that did and now are coming to pass at this very present time we are living in. The wake-up call is to stimulate the people to be prepared spiritually and physically. In what way they are to be prepared will be discussed in Chapter 4 of this book.

What is Eschatology? Webster's Dictionary defines Eschatology as that branch of theology or doctrines dealing with death, resurrection, judgment, immortality, etc.[1] The Nelson's Illustrative Bible Dictionary defines Eschatology even clearer: it is the study of what will happen at the end of history, particularly the event known as the Second Coming of Christ. The word comes from two Greek words, "eschatos" (last), logos (study) - thus its definition as "the study of last things." So that the author concludes with her understanding of Eschatology as being the study of things that will happen in the last days leading up to the second coming of Christ.[2]

---

1. Guralnik, David, Chief Editor, Webster's New World Dictionary, Ohio: William Collins Publishers, Inc., Copyright, 1979.
2. Nelson, Thomas, Nelson's Illustrated Bible Dictionary, General Editor, Herbert Lockyer, Sr., Tennessee Thomas Nelson Publishers, 1986 Pg. 351.

Part of the study of Eschatology is highlighted in the Book of Revelation. The Book of Revelation is the Apocalyptic Literature in the Bible in that the Apostle John was given a revelation of things to come and was told by Jesus Christ in a vision to write them down. The Nelson's Illustrative Bible Dictionary describes "Apocalyptic Literature" as a special kind of writing that arose among the Jews and Christians to reveal certain mysteries about heaven and earth, humankind and God, angels, demons, the life of the world today, and the world to come. The word "Apocalyptic" comes from the Greek word, "apocalypse" meaning "revelation."*[3] The author concludes the meaning of "Apocalyptic Literature" in a simple statement as God revealing mysteries of things to come through a believer spiritually and they are written down.

The study of Eschatology is hardly taught in churches today. If it is ever taught, it is taught by those individuals who God has anointed to teach it, such as, Min. Hilton Sutton, an anointed teacher of Eschatology. He has a ministry entitled, "Hilton Sutton World Ministries" in New Caney, Texas. The author has the privilege of being on his Issachar Team. He refers the task of this team to be the task of the Tribe of Issachar of the nation of Israel. Its task and spiritual gift was that it had an unusual insight into the political and end-time event situations. In other words, the children of tribe of Issachar had the understanding of the times so that they would know what the people of Israel ought to do to prepare herself for what is to come.

Dr. Hilton Sutton believes it is the responsibility of the body of Christ on his Issachar Team to be well informed and aware of the end-time events leading to the soon return of Jesus Christ so that they are able to share their information to alert the rest of the body of Christ to be prepared spiritually, doing the works that Jesus did as well as winning souls of unbelievers to the Christian faith. In other words, they are to prepare other people for the soon return of Christ.

---

3.   Ibid. Pg. 71.

Other teachers of Eschatology, to name a few, are Pastor John Hagee of the "Cornerstone Church in San Antonio, Texas; he is also President of the "Global Evangelistic Television." Itinerant Evangelist Marilyn Hickey of the "Marilyn Hickey Ministries" in Englewood, Co., the Hal Lindsey Ministries in Western Front, CA. Perry Stone Ministries, Grant Jeffrey Ministries and many others. Such Eschatology teachers, upon invitation, proclaim the signs of events happening today as manifestations of prophecies written in the Bible and share them at other churches as well as through their resource materials, audio tapes and videos they have produced.

Dr. Hilton Sutton said in his February, 2008 newsletter, "I pray that all followers of our Lord, Jesus Christ, are truly discerning the "Signs of the Times." Today's world news reveals the signs of the times and it is evident. We are now in the time of the end: the "Friday" of the believer's time for works (doing the Great Commission) has arrived and we should be getting ready to leave for Heaven. Jesus is coming and He's coming soon."

In chapter 1, the author will discuss what part of the end times we are living in as she uses Daniel's interpretation of Nebuchadnezzar's dream of the Metallic image and the events that are occurring today that tell we are living in the tail-end of the end times. She will confirm the manifestations of these events with scriptures in the Bible.

MEETING
IN THE AIR

FIRST RESURRECTION

Jesus Christ's imminent coming to rapture the remnant body of Christ can happen at any moment. Are you ready? You can be ready once you read this book.

CHAPTER 1

Past Time Of The Gentile Events Up To The Present End-Time Events

God's Purposes Of Knowing The Signs of the Times

There are five reasons why God wants us to know the signs of the times that tell of His Son, Jesus' coming for the Body of Christ:

1. To help us to be more aware of the events prophesied that are signs leading up to the coming of Jesus to catch away the believers in Christ. This event is called the 'rapture' which will be discussed in Chapter 3.

2. To help us to be ready spiritually for Christ as we continually walk by the Spirit and apply His written word in our lives, Luke 21:34-36 and 1 John 2:28-29.

3. To give us a sense of urgency to remain united with other believers of the Christian faith as a remnant body of Christ, Hebrews 10:24-25.

4. To give us a sense of urgency to prepare other people for Christ's coming when God calls all believers to do the ministry of reconciliation, 2Corinthians 5: 18-20.

5. To be aware of the adversities that have come and those that will come upon the earth so that we are not taken by surprise when they happen. Matthew 24:6.

Nebuchadnezzar's Dream Interpreted By Daniel

It is through Daniel's communion with God and prayer that Daniel, the prophet of God, was able to interpret Nebuchadnezzar's dream of a Metallic Image described in Daniel Chapter 2:14-28. It is by Daniel's interpretation of the king's dream that the body of Christ today can determine what part of the end-times the Church Age is about to come to an end and also determine what part of the end-times the body of Christ is living in right now.

The dream God gave to Nebuchadnezzar, even though he was a king of Babylon, a Gentile and not a Jew, was a prophetic dream concerning future Gentile kingdoms that will rule over the people of Israel, who God allowed to be in captivity, due to their rebellion against God and their idolatry serving other foreign gods during the Old Testament times. Daniel explained to the king that he dreamed of a metallic image of a man made of various metals of color. Each metal represented different Gentile kingdoms that will rule not only the nation of Israel, but the whole world. Daniel's Interpretation of the dream by the Spirit of God was as follows:

- **Head Of Gold** - represents the Babylonian Kingdom ruled by Nebuchadnezzar over the people of Israel about 625 B.C. - 539 B.C. (Daniel 2:38).

- **Arms & Chest Of Silver** - represents the Medo-Persian Empire. This kingdom conquered the Babylonian kingdom and also ruled over Israel about 539 - 330 B.C. (Daniel 8:20).

- **The Belly & Hips Of Bronze** - represents the Grecian Empire under the ruler-ship of Alexander the Great about 539 B.C. until his death in 323 B.C. at the age of 33; however, his kingdom over Israel and the Mediterranean area along with his Greek culture, was divided into four regions led by four Grecian generals. One general ruled over Greece, the other over Syria, another one ruled over Thrace or the Balkan countries, and the last general ruled over Macedonia. Even Palestine was under the rule of one of the generals as well, (Daniel 8:22) about 323-30 B.C.

- **The Skirt & The Two Legs Of Iron** - represents the Roman Empire under the leadership of King Caesar into the time of Jesus Christ's life on earth about 3 B.C. (Daniel 7: 7, 23). After the death of Jesus, about 33 A.D., about 37 years later in 70 A.D., a great army of Roman soldiers led by Titus, a Roman Centurion, came to destroy the city of Jerusalem and its temples, including Solomon's Temple.[*4] The invasion scattered the Jews and the Christian Jews of the early Apostolic Church to various nations throughout the earth.

About 364 A.D., the Roman empire divided into two Roman governments: The Papal government that oversees the countries in the Western division, such as Italy, Germany, Spain, France, etc. and most of the Mediterranean area of Europe, and the Grecian government that oversees countries in the Eastern division, such as Greece, Macedonia, Egypt, Iran, Iraq, the Balkan countries, Syria, Asia Minor, known as Turkey today and parts of the Mediterranean.

- **The Knees Of The Legs** - represents the time period of Jesus Christ's death burial and resurrection, the continuation of the division of the Roman Empire, and the beginning of the end-times and the Church Age.

1. The Early Church or The Apostolic Church Period - It was at this time period Christian Jews were in an upper room in Jerusalem and the Lord sent the Holy Spirit and baptized the 120 disciples of Christ with the fire of the Holy Spirit with the evidence of speaking in tongues, (Acts 2:2-4). Thereafter, the early Christian Jews were unctioned by the Holy Spirit to do evangelism and missionary work; some were teaching the gospel, some were prophets and others were apostles.

---

4.   Hurlbut, Jesse, L., The Story Of The Christian Church, Michigan: revised by the Zondervan Publishing House, copyright, 1970, pgs. 33,34

All were operating by the gifts of the Holy Spirit doing the works that Jesus did not only done in Jerusalem, but throughout Asia Minor, Greece, and parts of the Mediterranean region. Such missionaries who carried the gospel to these regions were Paul, Silas, Barnabas, Timothy and other missionary assistants, to name a few.

After the early Christian Jews and non- Christian Jews were scattered at 70 A.D. by the Roman Centurion, Titus, they later encountered severe persecution for exhibiting their Christian faith by the Emperors Decius about 249-251 A.D. and Diocletian about 284 - 305 A.D. The early church braved these persecutions and grew even stronger in spirit.*[5] In 313 A.D. Constantine formulated the Edict of Toleration Act which officially put an end to the persecution. Not until 323 A.D. did Constantine became an emperor and then Christianity was favored. However, Constantine was not a perfect emperor. He occasionally was cruel and tyrannical. He promoted Christianity not for the purpose of salvation, but to be ritualistic with decorative church buildings restored with its decorative stain glass windows and glamorous priestly garments for the clergymen.*[6] All the materialistic forms of godliness were present, but there was no power of the Holy Spirit operating in the restored churches that were destroyed by those emperors stated above who were persecuting the Christians. It was, however, under the Constantine Roman government that Christianity was the only religion for Rome, because he saw a figure of a cross in the sky with a phrase stating, "By this sign of the cross, you will conquer." When the Christians saw that Constantine was not only building decorative church buildings, but also formulating statues of saints and exalting them, they became afraid that Constantine was indulging in paganism and promoting his own belief that one is accepted by God through good works, instead of putting one's faith in Jesus Christ for acceptance. He was, however, the first Christian emperor who started the worship of God on

---

5   Ibid. The Story Of The Christian Church, pgs 44, 45.

6.   Ibid. Pg. 59

Sundays, instead of maintaining the Jewish tradition of keeping the Sabbath day on Saturdays.

During Constantine's reign in Rome, he became tolerant, both in temperament and from political motives, although he remained emphatic in his recognition of the Christian religion. He sanctioned no sacrifices to the images formerly worshiped and put an end to the offerings to the statue of the emperor. But he favored the toleration of all forms of religion and sought the gradual conversion of his subjects to Christianity through evangelization and not by compulsion.*[7]

After the reign of Constantine, his former ritualistic worship, paganism, decorative stained glass churches, and decorative garments, still worn by chief priests, popes and priests of today, were maintained into the Medieval Period about 600 A.D. to 1300 A.D. This was the Universal Church emerging into Catholicism.

During the Medieval Period, it was considered the Dark Ages in that the Universal Church (that grew from the early Apostolic church) was influenced and controlled by the papacy. Most Christians were forced to worship the Virgin Mary and other statue images of saints. The Clergy did ritualistic liturgy as well as emphasized good works to please God. Like Jezebel in the Old Testament and the Jezebel spoken of in Revelations 2:20, the Papal Church forced the people and Christians to bow down to pictures of saints. This became idolatrous. The teachings of the Papal Church became supreme over the teachings of the Word of God. The Jezebel spirit of persecution was evident during the wars of Crusades if papal laws were not obeyed. People were even burned at the stake if the Pope's rules were disobeyed. This was a period ruled by the Catholic Popes who demanded holiness through good works by human efforts. It was all a form of godliness, but without the power and light of Jesus Christ in the Catholic Church, it was considered a dead church spiritually, until God enlightened an individual by a biblical scripture that kept Christianity from being annihilated or extinguished. God gave the Monk and Teacher

---

7.   Ibid, The Story Of The Christian Church, pg. 66

in Germany named, Martin Luther a revelation as he read Romans 1:16-17 which says, "For I am not ashamed of the gospel of Christ, for it is the power of God to salvation for everyone who believes for the Jew first and also for the Greek. For in it the righteousness of God is revealed from faith to faith as it is written, "the Just shall live by faith." Martin Luther realized that anybody can be saved by putting one's faith in Christ and not by doing good works and ritualistic worship.

On this realization written in Romans 1:17, "the just shall live by faith," Martin Luther wrote the 95 Thesis and nailed them on the door of the Catholic Church for everyone to see in Germany. This spiritual enlightenment given by the Spirit of God within Martin Luther also was a spiritual enlightenment to other Christian activists as they read Martin Luther's teachings based on the revelation. Such activists as John Wycliffe, John Hus, John Calvin and William Tyndale and others. The Universal Church was emerging into the Reformation Period about the 16th to the 17th centuries. This time the Bible became the authority for the Christians who finally got to read it in their language dialect and not in the Latin Vulgate. Due to this enlightenment, many activists were persecuted; some even were burned at the stake by the Papal Clergy and hierarchy.

The Shins Of The Metallic Image And Ankles - Describes the Modern Day Church Period. The Reform Church Period led into the Modern Day Church around the 17th to the 19th centuries. It was the latter-day Universal Church or the Body of Christ who escaped out of the Catholicism Papacy rule and established their own churches, which started the Holy Ghost revivals that were sparked by activists, such as the Quakers; then later by John Westley, who established the Methodist Church, Charles Finney, D.L. Moody, etc. Missionary and evangelistic work returned in the 18th century and is still taking place today until Christ returns for the Body of Christ.

The 20th century churches, or the Modern Day Church Period led to the birth of other denominational and non-denominational churches throughout the world, such as evangelistic churches, Prophetic and Apostolic churches and other non-denominational Pentecostal and charismatic churches like that of the author's home church, "Christian Cultural Center" in Brooklyn, N.Y., A. R. Bernard, Pastor.

Another characteristic of the Church Age during the 20th century, occurring in the same period as a latter-day church are those churches that are lukewarm, the same characteristic of the Laodicean church in Asia Minor described in Revelations 3:14-22. There is no spirituality in these types of churches. There is much going on in them, but it is primarily worldly-oriented with its committees, societies and multiple clubs. There is an absence of spiritual heat of the Holy Spirit. Revival meetings are held, but instead of waiting on the Lord for power, everything is done by human effort with hype-energy. Praising God in gospel music has become entertainment instead of true worship. The poor and the saintly are not wanted in such churches because their presence is a rebuke.*[8]

The Feet Of Iron And Clay - Daniel explained in Daniel 2:41-43 (in the revised NKJV), "Whereas you saw the feet and toes partly of potter's clay and partly of iron, the kingdom (divided Roman kingdom) shall be divided; yet the strength of the iron (the Old Roman Empire influence) shall be in it, just as you saw the iron-mixed with ceramic clay." Vs 42, "And as the toes of the feet were partly of iron and clay so the kingdom shall be partly strong and partly fragile." Vs 43, "As you saw iron mixed with ceramic clay, they will mingle with the seed of men; but, they will not adhere to one another, just as iron does not mix with clay." The feet of iron and clay of the metallic image signifies the tail end of the end times of the Church Age. Within the in-step of the feet of the image, signifies a period of events occurring in the mid 20th century. Nations of more strength and of Roman influence will make alliances with those nations that are weak economically, militarily and politically and look to other nations

---

8.   Larkin, Clarence, <u>Dispensational Truth</u>, Pennsylvania, U.S.A.: Rev. Clarence Larkin Est. Publishers, copyright, 1920, pg. 131

for stability. Therefore, alliances such as NATO (The North Atlantic Treaty Organization), formed on April 4, 1949, and 17 nations signed this agreement for economic and military assistance.*[9] T he U.S.A., France, Italy, United Kingdom, Canada, West Germany (joined in 1955), the Netherlands, Belgium, Luxenbourg, Iceland, Portugal, Spain (joined in 1992), Czech Republic, Hungary and Poland (joined in 1999), Greece and Turkey (joined in 1982); the Benelux Agreement was formed on June 8,1948.*[10] Three European nations were involved in this agreement: Belgium, the Netherlands and Luxenbourg. This agreement coordinated their domestic economic and financial policies; the ECC or the Economic Community Commonwealth or known today as the Economic Common Market or the European Union that was formed on March 25, 1957. This organization was formed out of the initiation of forming the Treaty of Rome. The members of the EU are Belgium, Denmark, France, West Germany, Ireland, Italy, Luxenbourg, Netherlands, United Kingdom, and Greece (was voted in on May 28, 1979; but membership was enforced on January 1, 1981). This organization was also formed for political and military as well as for economic stability reasons. According to Daniel 2:43, just as the ten toes of the image of clay and iron did not mix or stick together, so some leaders of nations will break their agreement with their allies because of some disagreement of some kind.

Theologians and the author believe the ten toes of the metallic image represent the ten confederate nations of the EU. The EU will be considered the revived Roman Empire governing during the Great Tribulation Period and led by the ruler-ship of the Anti-Christ who will assign 10 kings of the EU over 10 confederate nations or regions.

The in-step of the feet of the metallic image also signifies the Church Age coming to a close. It is at this time, the believers in Christ sense the nearness of Christ's coming for the Body of Christ; yes, His coming is even at the door. However, before Jesus comes for His church at the

---

9.   Google computer Search, North Atlantic Treaty Organization, from the U.S. History
     Encyclopedia.
10. Willmington, H.L., Signs Of The Times, Illinois: Tyndale House Publishers, Inc., 3rd
     copyright, 1983, pgs. 98 - 100.

Rapture event, certain things must come to pass. They will be discussed as other latest signs that tell we are living in the tail end of the end times that are occurring during the in-step of the feet of the metallic image. One can conclude that since events that are occurring at the in-step of the feet of the metallic image, it indicates that the times of the Gentile over Israel is coming to an end at the end of the Great Tribulation. Already the stage is being set for the Great Tribulation to begin. This will be discussed in Chapter 5 of this subject area.

The Stone Cut Out Of The Mountain - In Daniel 2:44 the scripture reads, "And in the days of these kings the God of heaven will set up a kingdom which shall never be destroyed and the kingdom shall not be left to other people, it shall break in pieces and consume all these kingdoms, and it shall stand forever, vs.45.

"Inasmuch as you saw that the stone was cut out of the mountain without hands that it broke in pieces the iron, the bronze, the clay, the silver and the gold ..." Just as each Gentile kingdom that the metallic image represented did not last, so the Revived Roman Empire with the Anti-Christ as its leader during the Great Tribulation will not last. It will be put to an end at the Battle of Armageddon when Jesus will destroy the Anti-Christ army and his allies at Jesus' Second Coming. Jesus will set up His Millennial Kingdom that will last for 1000 years and the Kingdom of God will last forever after the Millennial Age into the Perfect Age, Revelation chapters 20 -22. The stone symbolizes the Kingdom of Jesus Christ or the Kingdom of God when thrown, it will and has destroyed the Gentile kingdoms that ruled and controlled not only Israel, but the world.

CHAPTER 2

OTHER LATEST SIGNS OF THE TIMES THAT TELL WE'RE LIVING IN THE LAST DAYS

Prophecies spoken by Jesus Christ in Matthew 24:3-14

The following latest signs have already manifested as Jesus Christ prophesied in Matthew 24:3-14 : " As Jesus sat on the Mount Olives, the disciples came to Him privately saying, "Tell us, when will these things be? What will be the sign of your coming and of the end of the age?" Jesus answered, "Take heed that no one deceives you. For many will come in My name saying I am the Christ and will deceive many." This prophecy has come to pass. One example of this is the Unification Church founded by Sun Myung Moon in 1954 in S. Korea and was brought to New York City, N.Y. His concept of Jesus was that Jesus was a perfect man, but was not God. He teaches that Jesus is the son of Zechariah. He was not born of a Virgin. Myung Moon continued to say that Jesus' mission was to get the Jews to support Him, find a perfect bride and begin a perfect family. Moon said the mission of Jesus failed. He said Jesus did not resurrect physically. Moon teaches that the second coming of Christ was fulfilled in Sun Myung Moon who is superior to Jesus and will finish Jesus' mission on earth.*[11]

As you can see Myung Moon's concept of Jesus and His mission does not comply with who Jesus is in the Holy Bible. Myung Moon claims himself to be the incarnate of the second Christ. Another example of this is the Jim Jones ministries. Many followers of his ministry believed

---

11. Bjornstad, James, Dr. And Staff, Christianity, Cults And Religions, a folded mini panel chart, California: Rose Publishing Co., copyright, 2005.

he was the Christ incarnated. Those who sat under his teachings were seduced to commit suicide by drinking poisonous fruit punch at a retreat camp meeting in the 1970s. Some of the members managed to escape from his ministry before they went to the camp meeting. This information was obtained from computer research and broadcasted in the news media in 1978. Matthew 24:6, "And you will hear of wars and rumors of wars. See that you are not troubled; for all these things must come to pass; but, the end is not yet." There were civil wars that have increased during the course of Gentile history since the death of Jesus Christ. Naming a few, the American civil war between the Southern states and the Northern states, civil wars going on in Iraq today, also in different parts of Africa against apartheid enforced by the police force. Wars increased from the days of the Crusade in the 14th century to the French Revolution in 1794; from the American Revolution of 1776 against England under the ruler-ship of King George III; from World War I in 1917 to World War II in 1939. America is presently at war with the terrorist extremists in Iraq and in Afghanistan.

This war is considered to be a religious war between Muslim extremists and the democratic government of America and its traditional values. Vs. 7, "For nations will rise against nations (ex. civil wars between native people in that nation) and kingdoms against kingdoms (ex. democratic government kingdoms against the communistic and dictatorship kingdoms). And there will be famines, pestilence and earthquakes in various places." Famines have increased, afflicting such places as the Sudan and parts of Africa. Pestilences have increased, such as, HIV-Aids, influenza, bird flu, salmonella, measles, polio, malaria, T.B., etc. Earthquakes are occurring in various places such as, California, Indonesia, India, and the recent one in China and in Afghanistan.

Vs. 8, "All these are the beginning of sorrows."

Vs. 9, "Then they will deliver you up to tribulation and kill you and you will be hated by all nations." Persecution and martyrdom increased from the time of the Apostolic Church in Jerusalem and in Asia Minor with the church of Smyrna after the resurrection of Jesus Christ until today. Christians in countries like China, Iraq and in other Communistic and dictatorship countries, are being persecuted because of their faith in Jesus Christ.

Vs.10, "And then many will be offended, will betray one another and will hate one another." Today one can't trust those individuals who would make an agreement with him or her and later, the agreement is broken unknowingly by either one of the partners. This offends the person who tried to keep the agreement. Those people who do not uphold or do what is right, hate those individuals that desire to do right.

Vs.11, "Then many false prophets will rise up and deceive many." Cult religions led by false prophets and teachers, teach false doctrines not written in the Holy Bible. Some false doctrines twist and disrespect the Word of God. A couple of these cults only accept Jesus Christ as a prophet. but not God in the flesh; such as, the Jehovah Witnesses and the Islamic religions. Many other cult religious sects do not believe that Jesus Christ was and is the incarnate of God or God in the flesh who came down from heaven by way of the Holy Spirit through the Virgin Mary.

Vs.12, "And because lawlessness will abound, the love of many will grow cold." We reflect on the shootings that had occurred on college campuses like at Virginia Tech and at the University of Illinois. The removal of prayer, Bibles from the library shelves and the Ten Commandments from Public Schools and public places have opened the door for vandalism, disobedience to authority, and the study of the New Age philosophy curriculums that encourage that homosexuality is okay, encourage teenage boys to wear condoms and encourage girls to take birth control pills to prevent sexually transmitted diseases. There are some Public Schools, especially in Greenville, N.C., that have introduced prayer and studying the Bible as a historical literature, without evangelizing, to dispel the New Age philosophy.

There are a variety of other lawless activities that are still occurring today; traffic laws are being violated, cheating is still taking place on tax returns, people continue to rob other innocent people, as well as banks.

All of these incidences cause people's hearts to grow cold with fear. Love is waxed cold towards people you can't trust and do not want to do right. That is why Jesus said to pray for your enemies and overcome evil with good. Jesus said let not your heart be troubled neither let it be afraid. Why did Jesus say this? He said this so that we as His disciples can live life with a peace of mind when we cast our care on Him. Jesus wants us to live life in good health physically and mentally with no worry.

Vs. 13. "He who endures to the end, shall be saved." That is, anyone who endures the circumstances of this world system without being affected by it, shall be saved from the powers of the enemy and be counted worthy to be in the rapture. Vs. 14. "And this gospel of the Kingdom will be preached in all the world as a witness to all the nations, and then the end (of the Church Age) will come," This piece of scripture has already manifested. The gospel is increasingly being preached by the five-fold ministers all over the world. Missionaries near and far are establishing churches and spreading the gospel of Jesus Christ. Today, the gospel is being spread by way of radio, television, computer web sites, books, CDs, videos, cassette tapes, through gospel music, and by ordinary people of Christ acting as ambassadors for Christ within their own neighborhoods.

Prophecies Spoken By The Apostle Paul

The Apostle Paul instructed Timothy, his student of the gospel, that there will come an apostasy in the last days of the Church Age. He said to Timothy in 2Timothy 3:1-7 and verses 12-14 (NKJV), "But know this, that in the last days perilous times will come: for men will be lovers of themselves, lovers of money, boasters, blasphemers, disobedient to parents (there is a law today against parents spanking their children. That is why by this law, such rude children can get away with anything and it allows children to overrule the authority of their them); unthankful, unholy, unloving, unforgiving, slanderers, without self-control, brutal, despisers of good, traitors, headstrong, haughty, lovers of pleasure rather than lovers of God, having a form of godliness; but denying the power. And from such people turn away."

Vs. 6- 7, "For of this sort are those who creep into households and make captives of gullible women loaded down with sins led away by various lusts, always learning and never able to come to the knowledge of the truth."

The scriptures above reveal what is happening today; we are definitely living in the last days. A few examples to verify what the scriptures above are revealing; such as, people who are addicted to winning easy money at the casinos and playing the lottery, and those people who overcharge customers enormous prices for a product just to make more money; these people are lovers of money. People who are poor and will steal to get money without working are also people who are lovers of money. Money has become an idol. Under the New Age religion one of their beliefs is that there is no such thing as evil. Whatever one thinks is right, is right in one's eyes or thinking. What a Christian discerns by the Spirit of God as being good and evil, a New Ager sees everything as right based on whatever one thinks is right. There is no absolute morality. In other words, what is truth to a New Ager? What is good? Satan is viewed as an angel, a being, a great and mighty planetary consciousness. He is not thought of as Satan who leads a being to sin and wrongdoing, as Christianity teaches. Man is his own Satan representing the collective thought- form of all those negative energies which man has built up and created. Man is his also his own salvation if one can approach this collective thought-form with love, without fear. Then one can go beyond this shadow and see the true angel of light that is there seeking to bring light to man's inner world. *[12]

This type of false thinking is not only a form of apostasy that Paul speaks of, that would occur in the last days, but this type of thinking opens the door to lawlessness and to the concept that good is bad bad is good.

---

12. Martin, Walter, "The Kingdom Of Cults", Minnesota: Published by Bethany House Publishers, revised copyright, 2003, pgs. 416 & 422.

There is no such thing as moral values according to the New Ager thinking. What one thinks is bad may be good in another's thinking. And what one thinks is good, may be bad in another's thinking,according to a New Ager's philosophy.

Another activity that Paul said would occur in the last days is that many people will have the form of godliness, but they won't have the Holy Spirit's power operating in them. Lukewarm churches and cult religions may fall into this category. The Spirit of God said through Paul from such religious people in these institutions, turn away.

In Vs 10-11, Paul compliments Timothy for following his teachings when confronting the apostasy in his community. Paul said, "But you (Timothy) have carefully followed my doctrine, manner of life, purpose, faith, long suffering, love, perseverance, persecutions ... And out of them all the Lord delivered me."

In Vs.12-14, Paul warned Timothy and other believers, and even warns believers today, "Yes, and all who desire to live godly in Christ Jesus, will suffer persecution. But evil men and imposters will grow worse and worse deceiving and being deceived. But as for you (Timothy and believers today) continue in the things which you have learned and been assured of knowing from whom you have learned them." Paul was encouraging not only Timothy, but the believers of the body of Christ today to abide by the Holy scriptures and to continue in the faith in Jesus Christ.

In Romans 1:24-32 (NKJV) that in the last days, "God will and has given up sinful man to uncleanness in the lusts of their hearts, to dishonor their bodies among themselves, who exchanged the truth of God for a lie and worship and served the creature rather than the Creator. For this reason God gave them up to vile passions. For even their women exchange the natural use for what is against nature; likewise, also the men leaving the natural use of the women, burned in their lust for one another; men with men committing what is shameful and receiving in themselves the penalty of their error which was due." Those who believe in reincarnation, especially those who are in the New Age and Eastern religions, worship creatures, carved animals and other figures made from the earth. They honor these animals and carved idols, instead of the God, the Creator, because they believe that these idols represent the saints who have died.

God also gave up men and women to their reprobate minds for those indulging in homosexuality, fornication and other immoral heterosexual activities. God allows the consequences of such practices to be used as a penalty that is due them, which today is the disease called HIV-Aids, syphilis and other sexually related diseases to occur. If such people do not repent of their lifestyle of immorality, they face the judgment of God along with those who support their lifestyle. For example, the news media recently reported that the courts in New Jersey and in California have passed a law in support of same sex marriages. Some Public Schools in New York City and in other states, with the exception of Greenville, N.C., have reading curriculums that teach students that having intimate relations with the same sex person and forming a family is okay. The Liberal Democratic Party does not stand against the lifestyle of the homosexual. It is the individual's choice to live that lifestyle and that they have the right and privileges to have healthcare and a good job. The author believes everyone should be employed and have healthcare, as long as the homosexual and other fornicators obey the rules of the job and do not impose their sexual lifestyle on any employee or student.

God, who is a Spirit being, is a God of love and a God of justice. He is a God who loves sinners and wants them to live a healthy and prosperous life. He gives prostitutes, homosexuals and fornicators a choice of life or death; they choose life if they repent and give up their immoral sexual lifestyle. God has made a way for them to overcome their bondage of sexual immorality and that is through the acceptance of His Son Jesus Christ who died for their sins of sexual immorality. Through Jesus Christ's Spirit, a sinner receives eternal life on earth and in heaven. He or she becomes righteous, justified as if he or she has not committed any sin. Hopefully by the reading of this subject matter, prostitutes, homosexuals and fornicators will come to repentance and accept Jesus as their Savior and Deliverer. It is the Spirit of Jesus that can adjust their sexual lives and deliver them from prostitution, homosexuality and fornication, to having a normal heterosexual relationship in friendship or in marriage. John 3:16-17(NKJV) says, "For God so loved the world that He gave His only begotten Son, Jesus that whoever believes in Him should not perish but have everlasting life." "For God did not send His Son into the world to condemn the world, but that the world through Him might be saved. 1John 5:12(NKJV) says, "He who has the Son has life; he who does not have the Son of God does not have life."

This is not talking about those who have been living an upright sexual life, but have contracted HIV-Aids by way of inheritance or by blood transfusions. God, by His mercy, through the prayers of the afflicted and other supportive Christians, and by medication, can overcome the disease by faith. Should they die of the disease as Christians, they shall still live in heaven. Nevertheless, those who desire to continue their immoral sexual habits are warned in Vs. 32, God said, "Those who knowing the righteous judgment of God that those who practice such things are worthy of death, not only do the same, but also approve of those who practice them." In other words, those government officials and supervisors of other institutions who know the law of God and yet practice immoral acts, as well as approve those who do immoral acts, shall also suffer God's judgment.

One Other Sign That Tells Of The Closeness Of Jesus' Secret Coming

Before the rapture event occurs, which will be discussed in depth in Chapter 3, certain things must also come to pass and they tell of Jesus' close return for the Church Body:

1. The author already spoke in Chapter 2 what Jesus has said in Matthew 24:14, "And this gospel of the kingdom will be preached in all the world as a witness to all the nations and then shall the end come

(the end of the Church Age; as well as the end of the Gentile rule and control of the world after the Battle of Armageddon.) As you can see, many today are turning to the Christian faith because of the spread of the gospel of the kingdom through the media communication - through books, tapes, CDs, through preachers, missionaries and other believers in the faith. God is preparing the Body of Christ for a greater outpouring of the Holy Spirit or a greater outpouring of His Glory. In some parts of the world in churches and in neighborhoods, the outpouring of God's glory has already started, such as in parts of South Africa with the ministry of Evangelist Rheinhard Boonke. In China, ordinary Chinese people get together to worship Jesus Christ in their underground churches despite the dictatorship government. The glory of God is so intense until the people worship the Lord until they are drunk in the Holy Spirit from sun up to sun down. God's glory is even manifested at the healing crusade of Todd Bentley in Lakeland, FL.*[13] There is also an outpouring of God's glory at Benny Hinn's healing crusades where manifestations of God's glory are experienced by any believing Christian group who, by faith, desires more of the Lord's presence and intimacy. The author believes that a revival will take place in America and in other parts of the world, not just in specific places of the world. The revival must take place before the rapture event occurs.

Those churches in the world, especially in America, that have not yet experienced the outpouring of God's glory, need first to be purged, purified and refined in preparation for this experience. God would do this by the fire of the Holy Spirit within each believer as he or she overcomes persecution, trials and tribulation Jesus says every believer will encounter. Jesus, although He was the Son of God, learned obedience by the things He suffered, Hebrews 5:8 (NKJV). Through the trials and persecutions, a believer learns to exercise patience (and also trust in the Lord for deliverance) when his or her faith is being tested, James 1:3 (NKJV).

---

13.   Wilson, Darren, Finger Of God, A commentary on DVD, California: Wanderlust Productions, 2006, Fourth selection on the menu entitled, "World On Fire".

The author believes that the Lord is going to either chasten or get rid of pastors or prophets and other ministerial leaders who are not equipping the saints for the ministry of reconciliation. These leaders should be teaching them how to apply the word of God to their everyday lives and disciplining and developing them to be spiritually mature. Out of their own greed, some leaders are just interested in the amount of funds that are being raised for the offering. Chairpersons of committees in some churches seek to raise funds by sponsoring trips to the casinos, giving hat sales, playing bingo and bridge for money, etc., instead of trusting God as their source to give such leaders and chairpersons wisdom to get wealth. Wealth can come from donations given to the ministry via biblical teaching conferences, registration donations for conferences in which a freewill offering is given; as well as giving musical or gospel concerts in which monies can be obtained as a profit from ticket sales or a free will offering can be collected. The goal of any minister should not be to make money, but to equip, teach and edify the body of Christ for the glory of God.

If the people of God will allow themselves to be led by the Spirit of God, then God will supply their needs financially and materially to get the job done according to his riches and glory and in His time.

In 1Peter 4:17 (NKJV) says, "For the time has come for judgment to begin at the house of God; and if it begins with us first, what will be the end of those who do not obey the gospel of God?" You sometimes hear on the news media about religious leaders engaging in some form of sexual immorality with children and that the divorce rate has increased among Christian couples, because of infidelity and domestic abuse. Unless there is repentance, God will expose such ministers publicly and cause their ministry to cease.

True repentance to God would restore their ministries and their marriage relationships as well as their emotional stability. We should thank God that He is a God of a second chance. God is cleaning up His churches today. The things that shouldn't be occurring within the church body are either going to be corrected or eliminated by God from the pulpit to the congregation.

The author believes that after the refining of the church body of Christ, especially in character, God will intensify His glory within the prepared vessels of the believers. Such believers long to have more of God's love and presence. They long to experience having the fire of the Holy Spirit operating in them so they can do the works that Jesus did when He walked the earth and do even greater works if they believe in the name of Jesus, John 14:12. The world's greatest evangelism and the gifts of the Holy Spirit will be more prevalent in the last days with the redeemed body of Christ. Many in prostitution who accept Christ will be saved, and those who walk in darkness will come to the light of Christ reflected within the believers of the church body, as described in Isaiah 60:1-3. The author believes that there will be a deeper worship of God by the Holy Spirit like the worship David expressed in the tabernacle.

The move of God's glory throughout the earth in our churches marks the beginning of another wave of His revival by His Holy Spirit that will affect the communities in our nation and in other nations. No one knows how long the wave of the Holy Spirit revival will last, but know this, when you see revival happening in the world and especially in America, the next event is the rapture of the redeemed universal church body of Christ.

If you wish to see how God's glory is moving in different parts of the world, refer to the DVD entitled, "The Finger Of God," a commentary by the Journalist of gospel events, Darren Wilson. You'll see how ordinary people are hungry for Jesus' as they worship Him in song and obey His word in the Bible. They are motivated by His love as the gifts of the Spirit are operating through them. The DVD can be purchased for a donation of $20 at the Sid Roth T.V. ministry, "It's Supernatural" P.O. Box 1918 Brunswick, GA., 31521.

CHAPTER 3

THE RAPTURE EVENT

Webster's Dictionary defines "rapture" as being carried away in body or spirit.*[14] The Greek word for "rapture" is "harpazo" which means to snatch away. "Harpazo" was translated into the Latin Vulgate Bible for rapture in 1Thess. 4:17 as "rapiemur"- to carry off or to snatch out.

Although the word itself is not in the English Bible, there are certain terms used in the Bible to define "rapture." 1Thess. 4:17 says, "We which are alive and remain shall be "caught up together" with them (the risen dead) in the clouds to meet the Lord in the air." In biblical terminology, "rapture" is referred to the term, "caught up together"; in 2Thess 2:1 "rapture" is referred to the term, "gathering together to Him" and lastly, in 2Thess. 2:7, "rapture" is referred to the term, "He is taken out of the way." This term means that when the Holy Spirit carries away the body of Christ with the help of angels, then Satan's messenger, the Anti-Christ can be revealed. The Holy Spirit will still remain on the earth throughout the Great Tribulation to be with the Tribulation saints outwardly with the anointing upon them, but not in them.

The presence of the Holy Spirit only abides within the church body before the rapture, but not after the rapture. The way the Holy Spirit related to the prophets in the Old Testament with the anointing upon their souls and physical body, (but not within their human spirit), is the way the Holy Spirit will relate to the Tribulation saints during the Tribulation Period.

---

14. Guralnik, David, Chief Editor, Webster's New World Dictionary: Ohio: William Collins Pub, Inc. copyright, 1979, pg 1177

The Purposes Of The Rapture Event

The purposes of the rapture event are as follows:

1. To fulfill Christ's promise to return and receive the saints to Himself, John 14:2-3 (N.L.B.). Jesus says, "There are many rooms in my Father's house and I am going to prepare a place for you. If this were not so, I would tell you plainly. When everything is ready, I will come and get you so that you will always be with me where I am ... ."

2. To receive judgment for our works done in the body of Christ. Paul said in 2Cor. 5:10, "For we must all stand before Christ to be judged. We will each receive whatever we deserve for the good or evil we have done in our bodies."

3. The body of Christ would be preserved in heaven to reign on earth with Christ after the Battle of Armageddon. Rev. 5:10 (NLB) says, "And you have caused them (saints) to become God's Kingdom and His priests and they will reign on the earth.

4. To resurrect the dead and the living in Christ from among the wicked. Philip. 3:20-21 (NKJV) says, "For our citizenship is in heaven from which we also eagerly wait for the Savior, the Lord Jesus Christ, who will transform our lowly body that it may be conformed to His glorious body according to the working (of the Holy Spirit) by which He is able even to subdue all things to Himself."

5. To change our mortal corrupt bodies into immortal incorruptible bodies or glorified bodies. 1Cor.15:53 (NLB) says, "For our perishable earthly bodies must be transformed into heavenly bodies that will never die."

6. To enable us to escape the Great Tribulation. 1Thess. 5:8-9 (NLB), "But let us who live in the light think clearly, protected by the body armor of faith and love and wearing as our helmet the confidence of our salvation." Vs. 9, "For God decided to save us

through our Lord Jesus Christ, not to pour out His anger on us."
In other words, God did not appoint to the body of Christ to live
through His judgment of the Great Tribulation intended for the
wicked world.

The Seven Raptures That Include The Raptures
In The Past And Future

There are seven raptures that include the raptures that have
occurred in the past and raptures that will occur in the future. They are as
follows:

Rapture 1: In the Old Testament, Enoch was raptured alive,
because he walked and talked with God, Gen. 5:24 (NLB), "Enoch (He)
enjoyed a close relationship with God throughout his life. Then suddenly
he disappeared because God took him."

Rapture 2: Elijah, the prophet, was raptured by a whirlwind in a
fiery chariot with horses, 2Kings 2:11 (NLB), " As Elijah and Elisha (they)
were walking along and talking, suddenly a chariot of fire appeared drawn
by horses of fire. It drove between them separating them and Elijah was
carried by a whirlwind into heaven."

Rapture 3: In the New Testament, Jesus was resurrected and
ascended into the sky, Acts 1:9 (NLB), "It was not long after He (Jesus)
said this (about the endowment of the Holy Spirit) that He was taken up
into the sky while they (the disciples) were watching and He disappeared
into a cloud."

Rapture 4: In the near future, the body of Christ or the Remnant
Church of Christians who remained in the faith and were filled with the
Holy Spirit, either alive or asleep in the graves, will be raptured in a
twinkling of an eye. Those who are alive at the time of the rapture will not
see physical death. 1Cor 15:51-52 (NLB), "Not all of us will die, but we
will all be transformed. It will happen in a moment, in the blinking of an
eye when the last trumpet is blown."

Rapture 5: During the mid Tribulation, the rapture of the 144,000 evangelistic Jewish tribes that were sealed by the Holy Spirit occurs Rev. 14:1- 3(NLB) says, "Then I saw the Lamb standing on Mt. Zion and with Him (Christ) were the 144,000 who had His name and His Father's name written on their foreheads. This great choir sang a wonderful new song in front of the throne of God."

Rapture 6: The Tribulation saints (who are not the church body) are raptured before the judgment activities of the seven vials or bowls. It is prophesied in Rev. 7:9,14(NLB) by John who saw in a vision, "a great crowd too great to count from every nation, tribe, people and language standing in front of the throne and before the Lamb. They were clothed in white and held palm branches in their hands." Rev 7:14(NLB), "Then he (the elder, after asking who were these who are clothed in white? Where do they come from? Vs. 13), said to me (John), "These are the ones coming out of the great tribulation. They washed their robes in the blood of the Lamb and made them white. That is why they are standing in front of the throne of God, serving him day and night in His Temple ... ." This scripture is still informational or prophetic in Rev. 15:2(NLB), "I saw before me what seemed to be a crystal sea mixed with fire. And on it stood all the people who had been victorious over the beast and his statue and the number representing his name. They were all holding harps that God had given them." This scripture comes to pass when the Tribulation saints are seen in heaven in Rev. 19:1, 6-9 in preparation for the Marriage Feast as guests invited to the Marriage Feast.

Rapture 7: The last rapture event at the end of the second 3½ years of the Great Tribulation is the rapture of the two witnesses whom God anoints with the Spirit and power of Elijah and Moses. Rev. 11:1- 6 gives information or prophecy concerning the ministry of the two witnesses as prophets. These witnesses warned the people of their judgment if they were to yield to the dictates of the Anti-Christ and the proclamation of the second coming of Jesus Christ. Their ministering extend from the mid-Tribulation towards the end of the Great Tribulation, (a period of 1,260 days, 42 months or 3½ years). In Rev. 11:7-10, it indicates that the Anti-Christ and his 10 confederate team nations fight and kill the two witnesses in the streets of Jerusalem after 1,256½ days of ministering, or 3 days before their ministry officially ended. In Vs. 11-12, God revives the two witnesses and raptures them before the whole world to see. Those who witness this event were terrified. In Vs. 13, John envisions in the same hour the two witnesses who were raptured, and an earthquake that destroyed a tenth of the city, wherein 7000 people died. Those who didn't die in the earthquake gave glory to God in heaven out of fear for their lives, not necessarily from their hearts. The rapture of the two witnesses comes to pass between the events of the 6th and 7th bowls in Rev. 16:17.

What Will Occur At The Rapture?

1Corinthians 15:51-54(NKJV) says, "Behold, I tell you a mystery: we shall not all sleep, but we shall all be changed in a moment, in the twinkling of an eye at the last trumpet. For the trumpet will sound and the dead will be raised incorruptible and we shall be changed.

For this corruptible must put on incorruption and this mortal must put on immortality. So when this corruption has put on incorruption and this mortal has put on immortality, then shall be brought to pass the saying that is written, "Death is swallowed up in victory."

We know from these scriptures that 1) The rapture is a mystery in that it was not revealed to man in the past, nor was it ever known to man before. It is now being revealed to the body of Christ through Paul's revelation of it by the Holy Spirit; 2) During the rapture, for those who are alive in Christ, there is no physical death; 3) All believers who remain in the faith and are endowed with the Holy Spirit, shall be transformed in a moments time in the blinking of an eye. All believers will have resurrected immortal bodies that will never die. These mortal bodies must put on immortality in order to abide in heaven with Jesus;

4) The rapture will be instant. There will be no time to repent; every believer in Christ will disappear into thin air in an atomic second; 5) At the rapture, believers will be given a signal of a sound of a trumpet that only believers in Christ will hear, not the unbeliever. 6) The dead shall rise first.

The trumpet is sounded for the believers to get ready to exit out of the earth. This is why ministers and believers must inform one another of the next coming event called the "rapture." They are to prepare for it spiritually and physically - spiritually by being baptized with the fire of the Holy Spirit, (with the fruit of the Spirit operating), and physically by applying the word of God in life's situations as well as doing the works that Jesus did. This subject matter will be discussed in more detail in Chapter 4.

Those who died in Christ, their soul- spirit now living with Jesus in heaven, will come back for their glorified bodies that were buried in graves at a moment's time at the rapture. Paul said in 1Thess. 4:13-18(NKJV), "But I do not want you to be ignorant brethren, concerning those who have fallen asleep or died lest you sorrow as others who have no hope. For if we believe that Jesus died and rose again, even so, God will bring with Him those who sleep in Jesus (in other words, the spirits of the dead will come back with Jesus for their glorified bodies left in the graves and they will be raptured first.) For this we say to you by the word of the Lord that we who are alive and remain until the coming of the Lord will by no means precede those who are asleep (dead)."

"For the Lord Himself will descend from heaven with a shout with the voice of an archangel and with the trumpet of God. And the dead in Christ will rise first. Then we who are alive and remain shall be "caught up together" (or raptured) with them in the clouds to meet the Lord in the air. And thus we shall always be with the Lord. Therefore, comfort one another with these words." 7). At the rapture, there will be a reunion with loved ones who were deceased and with Jesus Christ, in the air as well as in heaven; 8) At the rapture, all believers will dwell in the Father's House that has many mansions. John 14:2 (NLB) says, "There are many rooms in my Father's Home and I am going to prepare a place for you. If this were not so, I would tell you plainly. When everything is ready, I will come and get you so that you will always be with me where I am." 9) Following the rapture, every believer will face the Judgment Seat of Christ, not for sin, for that was dealt with when one received salvation, but they will be judged for the works done here on earth. If such works were done by the leading of the Holy Spirit, believers will be rewarded with specific crowns. Works not led of the Spirit will not be rewarded, however, by the grace of God, the person will still be saved and remain in heaven.

Paul said in 1Cor 3:13-15 (NLB) to the saints in Corinth and to believers today, "But there is going to come a time of testing at the Judgment Day (or the Judgment Seat of Christ) to see what kind of work each builder (or believer) has done. Everyone's work will be put through the fire to see whether or not it kept its value. If the work survives the fire (of the Holy Spirit), the builder will be rewarded with a crown. It means his work was led of the Spirit of God. If the work is burned up (or work did not last), the builder will suffer great loss (or will not receive a reward); however, the builders will be saved; but like someone escaping through a wall of flames (or is saved just to enter the door of heaven).

The following are the 5 rewards of crowns a believer can receive for spirit-led works at the Judgment Seat of Christ:

Crown 1: The Victor's Crown - For those believers who endure and overcome the temptations and trials of life. James 1:12 (NKJV) says, "Blessed is the man who endures temptation for when he has been proved, he will receive the crown of life which the Lord has promised to those who love Him."

Crown 2: The Martyrs' Crown - For those believers who suffer persecution and death for the sake of righteousness or for preaching the gospel or for standing up for Jesus Christ promoting His teachings. Rev. 2:10 (NLB) says, "You will be persecuted for ten days. Remain faithful even when facing death and I will give you the crown of life."

Crown 3: The Elder's Crown - For those ministers who were called of God to be a Christ-like example and good stewards over God's people.1Peter 5:2-4 (NKJV) says, "Shepherd the flock of God which is amongst you serving as overseers, not for dishonest gain; but eagerly (or not for what you would get out of it financially); not as being lords over those entrusted to you; but being examples to the flock. And when the Chief Shepherd appears, you will receive the crown of glory that does not fade away.

Crown 4: The Crown Of Righteousness - For those believers who look for the rapture or the coming of Jesus and for those who seek the kingdom first and for His righteousness. Paul said in 2Timothy 4:7-8 (NLB), "I have fought a good fight, I have finished the race and I remained faithful. Now the prize awaits me - the crown of righteousness that the Lord, The Righteous Judge, will give me on the great day of His return. The prize is not just for me; but for all who eagerly look forward for His glorious return."

Crown 5: The Crown Of Rejoicing - This is for those in the body of Christ who do the work of an evangelist or who operates as an evangelist, the crown is given to anyone who won souls for Christ. In 1Thess. 2:18-19(NKJV) Paul said, "For what is our hope or joy or crown of rejoicing? Is it not even you in the presence of our Lord Jesus Christ at His coming? For you are our glory and joy." In other words, for what is Paul's hope, joy and receiving a crown of rejoicing for? Isn't it by the work of sharing the gospel that you've accepted and will stand before Jesus Christ at His coming. Paul said he took delight and joy in seeing them saved when they accepted the good news of Jesus Christ that he preached.

The Rapture Event Is Not Considered
The Second Coming Of Jesus Christ

The Rapture event is not considered the Second Coming of Jesus Christ. Here's why: (Compare the Rapture events in the left column with that of the Second Coming of Christ events in the right column.)

The Rapture	The Second Coming
Believers change to immortality (1Cor.15:53-54)	Believers of sheep nations remain mortal after the Great Tribulation, Matt. 25:31-40 & Rev. 14:14-16.
Church of believers are raptured before the Day of Wrath of God. 1Thess. 5:9; Rev. 4:1.	Day of Wrath comes upon all wicked men. Romans 1: 18, 32.
Believers go to the Father's House John 14:2-3.	Late mortal believers of the sheep nations remain on earth during the Great Tribulation. The Wrath of God will not affect them, Matt. 13:47-50.
No reference of Satan at the time of the rapture.	Satan is bound 1000 years after the Battle of Armageddon. Rev. 20:1-3.
Jesus comes for His own Bride secretly John 14:3; 1Thess. 4:16-17.	Jesus comes with His Bride, everyone will witness, Rev. 19:11-14.
Jesus comes suspended in air, 1Thess. 4:16-17	Christ comes to earth standing on Mt. Olives. Zech. 14:3-4.
Believers are rewarded crowns, James 1:12; Rev. 2:10; 1Pet. 5:1-4 2Tim. 4-8; 1Thess. 2:19-20	Late mortal believers of sheep nations are saved and reserved for the Millennial Age as their reward; for the goat evil nations, there will be no reward but they will be destroyed at the Battle of Armageddon and then in the lake of fire. Rev. 14:14-20; Rev. 19:11- 21; Matt. 25:31-40.

The Rapture	The Second Coming
Gentiles and Jews are judged as one in Christ, Gal. 3:28.	Gentiles and Jews are segregated, Rev. 7:3-4; Rev. 12:14; Ezek. 20:35-38
Great Tribulation begins after the rapture, Rev. 4:1; 1Thess. 5: 9.	The Millennial Kingdom occurs after the Great Tribulation, Rev. 20:4-6.
The whole earth is not judged and destroyed, Matt. 24: 6.	At the Millennial Age, the earth is repopulated with mortal believers living in peace and prosperity, Isa. 65:17-23, 27.
	After the Millennial Age, the whole earth is destroyed by fire and recreated into a New Earth and a New Heaven, 2Pet. 3: 10 -13; Rev. 21:1-4.

The Rapture Is A Pre-Tribulation Event Vs.
Mid and Post-Tribulation Events

Certain terms will be mentioned in this section of Chapter three such as, "The Tribulation saints," "Great Tribulation," "pre-tribulation," "mid-tribulation" and "post-tribulation." The tribulation saints are those people who did not accept Christ before the rapture and therefore, were not raptured with the body of Christ; they were left behind. After the rapture begins there is a seven year period of the Great Tribulation. It is during this period that evangelism continues by the 144,000 Jewish people as they spread the news about salvation through Jesus Christ. Many other Jews and Gentile people may decide to accept Jesus Christ in their lives; these are called Tribulation saints. They will not be considered the remnant Bride of Christ or the remnant Church. The Church body or Christians would have been already raptured before the seven year period of the Great Tribulation begins. The Tribulation saints will not encounter God's wrath the way the wicked unbelievers will encounter it, however, they will be persecuted by the Anti-Christ because of their faith in Jesus Christ, Rev. 6:9-11. If they stay faithful to Jesus until death, they will be rewarded with wearing fine robes of righteousness and take part in the marriage feast of Jesus Christ in heaven as invited guests, Rev. 19: 8-9. More will be discussed about the tribulation saints in Chapter 5.

The Great Tribulation or the Wrath of God is a short seven-year period that takes place right after the Rapture event. For the first three and a half years of the Great Tribulation, God permits a period of intense distress and suffering instigated by Satan through the Anti-Christ and his armies. During the second three and a half years which is during the mid-tribulation, God's wrath upon the wicked who refused to hear the gospel of the 144,000 Jews, becomes extremely intense and is expressed through seven trumpets and vials of great affliction upon the bodies of the wicked, e.g., water being poisoned, disasters in the heavens.

Pre-tribulation is defined as the period of events that occur before the Great Tribulation-such as the Rapture event. This event is considered a pre-tribulation event. The mid-tribulation is that period that occurs at the end of the first three and a half period and the beginning of the second three and a half of the seven year period of the Great Tribulation. The Post-tribulation is that period at the end of the seven year period of the Great Tribulation when the wicked people, the Anti-Christ and his armies, are destroyed by Jesus Christ and the saints by the fire of His presence at His second coming. The battle will be the Battle of Armageddon described in Rev. 19:11-21.

Some theologians believe that the Day of Wrath of God, described by the seven seals in Rev. 6, has already begun. The perilous events of many earthquakes, pestilences, famines, terrorism of wars between nations and kingdoms, people being persecuted and martyred for their faith in Jesus Christ, have increased since 1945 (taken from the Leaflet entitled, "The Third World War" by the Pastor of The Christian Assembly and Pentecostal Church in U.S.A. at www.cai.org/leaflets/ thethirdworldwar). Since these perilous events are getting worse, there are some theologians that feel that we are living in the times of the beginning of the Great Tribulation during the time of the seven seals events. Therefore, such theologians who think this way sense that the rapture will be a mid-tribulation event.

The above argument cannot be so for Jesus said in Matt. 24:6-7 (NKJV), " And you will hear of wars and rumors of wars. See that you are not troubled for all these things must come to pass, but the end is not yet. For nation will rise against nation and kingdom against kingdom. And there will be famines, pestilences and earthquakes in various places. All of these are the beginning of sorrows. Then they will deliver you up to tribulation (or persecution) and kill you and you will be hated by all nations for My name's sake." As you can see, what Jesus prophesied is intensifying in the last days. They are setting the stage for the same events that will happen in a worse way during the beginning and mid-tribulation described by the activities represented by the seven seals and seven trumpets in Rev. chapters 6 and 8. The theologians who believe that the rapture will occur after the mid-tribulation overlook the scripture in Rev. 4:1 in which Jesus tells John in a vision to "Come up here" in the Spirit so that Jesus can show John what must take place after John's ascension into heaven. This scripture describes John's experience of a rapture to happen before the future event of judgment activities that will happen to the wicked during the seven year period of the Great Tribulation.

Other theologians believe the church will live through the Great Tribulation event and be raptured after the Tribulation seven year period. Minister Roger Armstrong was such theologian who believed that the rapture of the church will be a post-tribulation event. Minister Armstrong, a minister of the gospel (as he called himself) in Southern California, attended an "End-Time Bible Prophecy Conference" in Redding, CA on March 3, 2007. 500 mixture of 500 ministers and pastors attended this conference also. With the exception of Min. Armstrong, other ministers and pastors believed that the second coming of Christ was presented as a two stage event. The first stage would be before the Great Tribulation and the second stage, Christ's second coming, would occur after the Great Tribulation. Three senior pastors verified those two stages with nine scriptures that indicated that the rapture will be a pre-tribulation event. Min. Armstrong proved that the resurrection or the rapture occurs after the tribulation and that it would be a post-tribulation event.*[15]

The author will only refer to two scriptures Min. Armstrong used to back his argument. Then the author will use scriptures and one other resource to prove that Min. Armstrong misinterpreted the scriptures in order to clarify that the rapture is a pre-tribulation event.

Min. Armstrong stated, "There is not a single scripture that specifically places the rapture before the Tribulation. So, we have to assume that God will take us out of this tribulation event because 1. God took Noah out of the flood; 2. The three Hebrews were delivered from the fiery furnace. They were not for both cases. They were carried through the tribulation;" 3. "The saying that since the church is not mentioned after the third chapter in the Book of Revelation, indicates that the church is raptured. Using this logic, we can also say that hair on the head of people is not mentioned after the third chapter in the Book of Revelation, so this proves that all of these people did not have hair. In fact, all of Revelation is directed to the church." (Scripture 1) - Min. Armstrong stated, "In Rev. 22:16 (NKJV), Jesus said, "I, Jesus, have sent mine angel to testify unto you these things unto the churches;" 4. "the saying that the timing of the rapture is linked to the timing of the Resurrection. The Resurrection happens at the last day,; not seven years before the end of the Age." Armstrong continued to say, "Jesus says four times in John 6:39,40,44,54 (scripture 2) that He will be raising people up at the last day. So we know the resurrection will be after the Tribulation in Rev. 20:4 because the tribulation martyrs are included in the resurrection. Resurrection and the rapture happens on the last day. Clearly, this again is a post-tribulation event.

---

15. Lindsey, Hal Ministries, <u>End-Time bible Prophecy Conference</u>, California: 2007, obtained from Lindsey's website, <u>www.westernfront.com</u>

The author's response to Min. Armstrong's interpretation of Rev. 22:16 is that the scripture he used was taken out of context from Rev. 22:6-17. In this passage of scripture, Jesus concludes with what He has revealed to the Apostle John. He was to write down Jesus' encouragement and warning to the churches in Asia Minor and to the churches that incorporate the body of Christ in Chapters 2 and 3. In Rev. 22:14, he said, "Blessed are those who do His commandments, that they may have the right to the tree of life, and may enter through the gates into the city." The body of Christ that is sealed and whose vessel is the temple of the Holy Spirit, does not live through the Great Tribulation. If this was the case, God would go against His word stated in 1Thess. 5:9 (NKJV) in which Paul said, "God did not appoint us (the body of Christ) to wrath (to suffer the Great Tribulation); but to obtain salvation through our Lord Jesus Christ." God would be going against His word in 2Thess. 2:7- 8 (NKJV) where Paul said, "For the mystery of lawlessness is already at work; only He (the Holy Spirit within the Body of Christ) who now restrains will do so until He (the church body of Christ) is taken out of the way (or raptured). Then the lawless one (Anti-Christ) to be revealed whom the Lord will consume with the breath of His mouth and destroy with the brightness of His coming (at the end of the Great Tribulation at the Battle of Armageddon).

In Rev. 22:17, Jesus calls His church His Bride saying, "The Spirit and the bride say, "Come." If Min. Armstrong considers the tribulation saints as part of the body of Christ, living through the Great Tribulation, his thinking errs. Though the tribulation saints accept Jesus as their Savior, they are sealed by the Holy Spirit outwardly and not inwardly like the Spirit indwells the body of Christ that is raptured. Again, the tribulation saints are not the church body. Rev. 7:14 says, "And he said to me, "these are they which came out of the tribulation and have washed their robes and made them in the blood of the Lamb. They have trusted in the message of the blood and are clothed in the righteousness of Christ." The great multitude of tribulation saints is separate company from the church body of Christ. They are like the Old Testament saints for they are saved after the rapture.*[16]

Just as the Old Testament prophets had the Holy Spirit upon them, so it is with the tribulation saints. That is why the body of Christ is distinguished from the tribulation saints; the body of Christ is redeemed by the Holy Spirit within them on earth. The tribulation saints are redeemed by the Holy Spirit after they are raptured towards the end of the 31/2 years of the Great Tribulation. Min. Armstrong did not make this distinction in his statements. Both groups of saints, however, are considered to be in the family of God through Christ . All will take part in the Marriage Feast and enter the New Jerusalem in heaven along with the 144,000 Jewish nations that are raptured during the mid-tribulation. All the saints would have been saved in the first resurrection, Rev. 19:1-9 and Rev. 20:4-5.

The author's response to John 6:39, 40, 44 and 54 is taken from the Dake's Annotated Reference Bible. It interprets the term," last day" to mean the last day of redemption of the righteous when their bodies will be fully redeemed. It gives 1Cor. 15:51- 53 as a reference to explain the redemption of the righteous bodies, "but we shall be changed in a moment, in the twinkling of an eye, at the last trumpet. For the trumpet will sound and the dead will be raised incorruptible; and we shall be changed. For the corruptible must put on incorruption and this mortal must put on immortality." The scripture tells that on their last day which is the rapture, their bodies will be redeemed. Their human spirits are already redeemed by the blood of the Lamb before the rapture.

Then there is the rapture of a different class of people called the tribulation saints. Their rapture will be considered their last day when the Lord will raise them up the author believes and other theologians will happen before the outpouring of intense judgment activities of God represented by the seven bowls or vials during the last 31/2 years of the

---

16. Dake Finis, Jennings, <u>Annotated Reference Bible</u>, King James Version Text, Georgia: revised Copyright, 1987 by Finis Jennings Dake., pg. 289, column 1 no. 4

Great Tribulation Period. Min. Armstrong does not make a distinction between the tribulation saints from the Church, (the body of Christ that is raptured before the tribulation saints are raptured), but he classifies them as still part of the Church, the body of Christ. His judgment of this is wrong. The righteous of the Church Age and the righteous of the Great Tribulation are two different groups raptured in two different periods, however, both raptures are considered the first Resurrection. In the second Resurrection, the wicked dead will be raised to face the White Throne Judgment and then after, they are cast into the lake of fire.

WHAT WILL ACTUALLY OCCUR
AT THE RAPTURE EVENT?

It was explained in Chapter three that those who have Jesus' Spirit (referred to as called the Holy Spirit) within their human spirit, and are living on earth, will be instantly changed into incorruptible, immortal and glorified bodies in a moment's time. In a twinkling of an eye, the Christians or the body of Christ will be drawn like a magnet drawing nails to Jesus Christ who will be suspended in the clouds to receive both those who were dead in Christ in the graves, as well as those Christians who will be alive when the Rapture occurs.

When the Rapture event occurs, imagine what will be like if you were one of those who did not accept Christ as your personal Savior and you were left behind. What would you experience seeing? For one thing, it would be in the news media around the world. It would be in the headlines of newspapers saying, "MULTITUDES MISSING, DISASTER STRIKES THE EARTH". The sudden removal of Christians around the world would cause a world-wide crisis, confusion and panic,; because of the incidences that would take place, such as:

- Driveless cars, buses, trucks and train wrecks
- Airplane crashes due to missing crew members
- Mass confusion on the radio and T.V. news medias

- Rampaging lawlessness crime and mobs that the police force would not be able to control
- Graves of the Christian dead opened and bodies resurrected.
- Packed churches of liberal religions and false cults seeking answers from their ministers.
- Families terrified and in shock over missing Christian family members. (Information taken from the "Tribulation Map Tract by Min. Leon Bates)

You are left behind and you are confused and panicking. What will happen next? The Bible says in Daniel 9:7 that a "world leader" will act as the savior of the world having the answer for all of the confusion in the world. He will seek to restore a temporary peace among the nations, even with the Arab nations. He will establish a seven year peace treaty with Israel. He will allow the Jews to rebuild Solomon's Temple. This will happen at the beginning of the seven year period of the Great Tribulation of God's judgment upon the wicked. During the mid-Tribulation, the world leader called the Antichrist, will destroy the Jewish worship of God in the temple and declare himself god in the temple with an image of himself in the temple as well,(Daniel 11:36-39). He will break the seven year peace treaty with Israel and begin to persecute and kill the Jews and those who decided to give their lives to Jesus Christ, because they refuse to worship him.

The Antichrist will be like another Hitler who was a former Nazi leader of Germany during 1943-1945. He too killed Jews by the thousands in gas chambers. The Jews call this mass killing, the Holocaust. The Antichrist may not use the gas chambers to kill his victims, but part of his weaponry will be the use of the guillotine for both the Jews and the tribulation saints who give their lives to Jesus Christ. He will force everyone to be under his control with his seal of 666 worn on the right hand or forehead of those who accept his rule out of fear. The tribulation saints who accepted Christ would rather be laughtered and their spirits live in heaven, than to take the mark of the beast and live in hell's fire forever.

Who wants to live during the Great Tribulation either as an unsaved person or as a tribulation saint? No one in their right mind would want to live during that period. It will be very difficult to be a tribulation saint, however, God's Spirit will sustain them and keep them in peace. At the end of Chapter five, it will explain how the unsaved person can avoid living in the Great Tribulation and be counted worthy to be in the Rapture when it occurs.

CHAPTER 4

PREPARATION FOR THE RAPTURE

The Responsibility Of The Holy Spirit To Prepare
The Body Of Christ

God cannot send Jesus to rapture the body of Christ unless the Universal Church of the body of Christ is cleansed, transformed and restored by the Holy Spirit. The Holy Spirit assists the church body to live in its spiritual potential by living by the fruit of the Spirit, doing the works that Jesus did and operating in the gifts of the Holy Spirit. In Acts 3:19–21 (NLB) Peter exhorts the members of the house of God by saying, "Now turn from your sins and turn to God." This passage of scripture is addressed to members of the body of Christ who have the Laodicean character or the lukewarm members of Christ who lost their first love of Jesus. The scripture is also addressed to churches whose members exhibit all forms of godliness, but do not operate by the power of the Holy Spirit. Such church members need to repent and return to their first love of the Redeemer, Jesus Christ.

Vs. 20 says, " Then wonderful times of refreshment will come from the presence of the Lord and He will send Jesus, your Messiah to you again;" that is, God's glory of His Spirit will indwell the body of Christ in a greater degree to be refreshed and empowered, then Jesus will come to get His Bride, the church body.

Vs. 21 says, "For He (Jesus) must remain in heaven until the time for the final restoration of all things as God promised long ago through His prophets." In other words, the Holy Spirit will bring about a revival within the Universal Church Body all over the world being led of the Spirit to do a quick work of evangelism with the love of Christ followed by signs and wonders as they operate in the gifts of the Holy Spirit. How long the revival will last in the last days, no one knows; however, when believers see the revival taking place all over the world, they are to look up for their redemption is near at hand to be raptured. Yes, even at the door.

The Responsibility Of The Believer To Prepare

It is the church body's responsibility to study the word of God at their local church Bible study or at a Bible institution if they so desire, or at a Bible Study group gathering outside their church or study on their own if they so desire with the help of the Holy Spirit. Once the Word of God is studied and/or heard, they should be able to apply the word of God in their life's situations, despite the circumstances being favorable or unfavorable.

Ephesians 6:11-18 instructs the believers to put on the whole armor of God so that they can withstand in the evil day and having done all, to stand. 2 Timothy 2:15 (KJV) encourages the believers, "to study to show thyself approved unto God a workman that needeth not to be ashamed rightly dividing the word of truth."

It is the five-fold ministers' responsibility to teach and equip the saints to do the work of the ministry of reconciliation. Ephesians 4:11-12 (NLB) says, "He (Jesus) is the one who gave these gifts to the church: the apostles, the prophets, the evangelists, and the pastors and teachers." Vs 12. "Their responsibility is to equip God's people to do His work and build up the church, the body of Christ, until we come to such unity in our faith knowledge of God's Son that we will be mature and full grown in the Lord, measuring up to the full stature of Christ."

2 Corinthians 13:14 encourages the believers to fellowship with the Holy Spirit when Paul gives the benediction to the saints in Corinth saying, "May the grace of our Lord, Jesus Christ, the love of God and the fellowship of the Holy Spirit be with you all."

Once we continue to fellowship with the Holy Spirit, the Holy Spirit will strengthen our human spirit and empower us, Christians. Our human spirit will be more sensitive to the move of the Holy Spirit within us when we fellowship with the Holy Spirit through praise and worship, praying in the Spirit in our native language or in a supernatural language called speaking in tongues as the Spirit of God gives the utterance; especially, when we intercede in prayer on behalf of someone or for ourselves, as well as fellowship with the Holy Spirit as we study the word of God. The more we learn how to recognize God's voice, the more we are less likely to make mistakes often. This takes practice. When we learn to get God involved in every situation of our lives, we will notice how much God will answer us through impressions in our spirit or through righteous thoughts that come from your spirit to your mind, or by an unction or by a still small voice.

Sometimes God can answer prayers through dreams and visions, through believers and ministers, through a child, in His word, in a book, or with a timely encouraging word on a bumper sticker. Sometimes God's answers to our prayers are not always instant. We need to give God a chance to work on peoples hearts to turn things around on our behalf before the answer is manifested. We must know that the moment we pray according to the will of His written word, God hears our prayers and He is working on it for our good. He will not answer though, if what we ask doesn't have our best interest at heart. Whenever or however God's answer comes, it can make a difference in someone's life and turn things around for the better.

In Galatians 5:16-18 (NLB), Paul says to the body of Christ, "I advise you to live according to your new life in the Holy Spirit. Then you won't be doing what your sinful nature craves." Vs. 17, "The old sinful nature loves to do evil, which is just opposite from what the Holy Spirit wants. And the Spirit gives us desires that are opposite from what the sinful nature desires." Vs.18, "But when you are directed by the Holy Spirit, you are no longer subject to the law (of the sin nature)."

This chapter will end with Paul exhorting believers not only in Corinth, but he was addressing Christians today concerning their preparation for the rapture. He said in 1Corinthians 15:58 (NKJV), "Therefore, my beloved brethren, be steadfast, immovable, always abounding in the work of the Lord, knowing that your labor is not in vain to the Lord." The author believes Paul was saying that we should be steadfast on the promises of God in good times or bad times, remain immovable from the faith, don't be easily persuaded by every wind of doctrine, and continue to trust God's word. Always use your natural talent(s) and spiritual gift(s) that will bring glory to Jesus. No matter how small or large the task led of the Holy Spirit, it is never overlooked by God.

CHAPTER 5

SIGNS SETTING THE STAGE FOR THE GREAT TRIBULATION

The author already mentioned in Chapter 1, one sign that is setting the stage for the type of government that will manifest during the mid-tribulation of the seven year period of the Great Tribulation will be the Revive Roman Empire. Many theologians and the author believe that the ten toes of iron and clay on the feet of the metallic image in the dream of Nebuchadnezzar represents 10 confederate nations that created an alliance to form the 1957 organization entitled, "The European Union." It was formed for economic stability and to establish a one world bank, as well as to establish (in the future) a one world government, which has not happened yet. The European Union will more likely be that world government during the Great Tribulation.

Three other signs are setting the stage for events to manifest during the Great Tribulation: 1. Presently, the Jews are returning to their homeland, Israel, since Israel became a nation on May 14, 1948. Thousands of Jews from Russia, Ethiopia, Bulgaria, Yemen, from other Middle Eastern countries like Iran and Egypt, E. Europe and some from America are returning back to Israel. The largest housing boom in Israel's history has and still is in progress with over 97,000 apartments under construction. Progress on the job front is less impressive, but the government plan claims it could produce 25,000 new jobs. *[17] God prophesied through Ezekiel that He would bring His people, the Jews,

---

17. Goodman, Hirsh, chief ed., The Jerusalem Report, Israel: Jerusalem Report Publications Ltd., June 13, 1991 issue, pg. 14 column 1.

from the nations He allowed them to scatter to when Titus, a Roman centurion, and his army invaded the city of Jerusalem in 70 A.D. In Ezekiel 36:24 (NKJV), it says, " I (God) will take you from among the nations, gather you out of all countries and bring you into your own land." In Ezekiel 36:22, God indicates that He is bringing the Jews back to their home not for their sake; but for His Holy name's sake to whom the Jews had profaned. His name would be hallowed before the eyes of the nations the Jews came from.

The author believes God is also bringing the Jews to their homeland to test their love for Him. During the beginning and mid- tribulation, their faith will be tested as to whether they will accept the Messiah, Jesus Christ as their personal Savior when they hear the gospel of salvation through Jesus Christ proclaimed by the 144,000 Jewish tribes. The 144,000 Jewish tribes will be the evangelists up to the mid-tribulation. The 144,000 Jews who are also sealed by the Holy Spirit in Rev. Chapter 7 will also minister salvation to the unregenerate Gentiles who are left behind after the rapture. After the 144,000 are raptured in Rev.14:1-5, in verses 6-11,3 angels prophesy to the people to turn to God followed by the two witnesses prophesied in Rev. 11:2-13 who will preach in the second half of the Tribulation.

Those Jews who have returned back to Israel from the four corners of the earth before the rapture event and have already accepted Christ, as their Messiah who had come to earth as a babe, ministered on earth as a prophet, did many miracles, died on the cross and rose again or is alive today, are called "Messianic Jews." They believe their Messiah or Meschua, their Savior, had already come, was resurrected and ascended to the right hand of God in heaven. Such Jews are considered Christian Jews as well today. Those Jews who accept Christ as their Messiah because of the gospel of Christ they heard, will take part in the rapture. They are considered to be one with the body of Christ of other believers that are not Jews. God said He would put His Spirit within the heart of Jews which can only happen when they accept Christ as their personal Savior. Ezekiel 36:26-28 (NKJV) says, "I (God) will give you a new heart and put a new spirit within you; I will take the heart of stone out of your flesh and give you a heart of flesh." Vs. 27. "I will put My Spirit within you and cause you to walk in my statutes, and you will keep my judgments and do them". Vs. 28., "Then you shall dwell in the land that I gave to your fathers, you shall be My people, and I will be your God." Those who have returned back to their homeland and have not accepted Jesus as their Messiah due to their belief that the Messiah had not come yet by the time of the rapture, will not take part in the rapture. They will be left behind to suffer in the period called Jacob's Trouble which is also called the period of the Great Tribulation, Jeremiah 30: 7. The author believes that after the rapture, many Jews and Gentiles are urged to receive Christ as their Savior up to the mid-tribulation and towards the end of the tribulation. Out of this tribulation group, God will raise up evangelists such as the 144,000 Jews sealed by the Holy Spirit with God's name written by an angel, Revelations 7:1-16. They are sealed to be set apart to do a divine work of salvation to the Jews and Gentiles who desire the Messiah in their lives. If they accept Christ, they shall be in heaven before the throne of God eventually. It will be very difficult to maintain the Christian faith during the Great Tribulation when the Anti-Christ and the Revived Roman Empire of the confederate nations will be in power. However, many of those who remain in the Christian faith amongst the Jews and the Gentile people or the tribulation saints, will be bold with the help and comfort of the Holy Spirit to face and endure persecution; even to face martyrdom.

Despite the fact that during the beginning and mid-tribulation, the Jews that still have not accepted Christ as their Messiah who had already come, God remains faithful to them and exhibits His grace and patience towards them as He protects them in the wilderness they run into from the persecution and military threat of the Anti-Christ and his army during the mid-tribulation.*[18] God has prepared in the wilderness near the Jordan area a refuge city called, 'Petra'. The refuge city is situated between Edom and Jordan and still exists today. Its temple buildings are carved into red mountainous cliffs. It was a great commercial centre in the days of King Solomon. In 105 A.D.,the Romans conquered the country and called the

---

18.   Revelations 12: 13,14 (NLB)

province Arabia Petra. When the power of Rome waned, Petra gradually fell into the hands of the Arabs and became completely lost to the civilized world in the seventh century and remained until it was rediscovered by Burckhardt in 1812.*[19]

One enters the city through a narrow winding defile or canyon from 12 to 40 feet wide. The sides are so tall and close together that it almost shuts out the blue sky. The sides of the entrance varies from 200 to 1000 feet. The length of the canyon is about 2 miles. Once inside the city, one would see other magnificent buildings, tombs and monuments.

The cliffs that surround the city are carved and honeycombed with excavations to a height of 300 feet above the floor of the valley. The excavations cut as they are out of different colored strata of the rock; such as, red, purple, blue, black, white and yellow, that becomes indescribable and overpowering to the beholder.*[20] So that when the mid-tribulation Jews represented as the "woman" (Israel) fleeing into the wilderness to escape from the hands of the "Avenger of Blood" (The Anti-Christ) mentioned in Revelation 12:13-14, will be protected in the City of Refuge, Petra, during the last 3 1/2 years of the Great Tribulation.

At Jesus second coming as King-Priest of the Armies of Heaven and His appearance is seen coming from the direction of the city of refuge, Revelation 1:7 says, "Behold, He is coming with clouds, and every eye will see Him, even they who pierced Him; and all the tribes of the earth will mourn because of Him. Even so, Amen." Matthew 24:30 says, "Then the sign of the Son of man will appear in heaven, and then all the tribes of the earth will mourn, and they will see the Son of Man coming on the clouds of heaven with power and glory." It is at Jesus' second coming that Jews who do not accept Him as their Messiah, begin to remorse over what they have done to Him; it is then that they will accept Him as their Messiah. Jesus as their King and all the saints

---

19. Larkin, Clarence, <u>Dispensational Truth</u>, Pennsylvania, U.S.A.: Rev. Clarence Larkin Est. Publishers, Copyright, 1920, pg.137.
20. Ibid

of heaven shall deliver them from the city of refuge after the Battle of Armageddon, praise the Lord!

2. The next stage that is set to happen during the Great Tribulation is that preparations today are underway to rebuild the Tribulation Temple. After Israel's victory in the sixth day war against the Arabs to regain the city of Jerusalem, the war was considered necessary before the building of a Tribulation temple.*[21]

Jack Van Impe, a teacher of Eschatology, refers to an article in the 'Time' magazine cover asking, "Time For A New Temple?" The in-depth story within the article revealed how Israeli Jews are planning ways to establish a new temple or establish a replica of Solomon's temple to continue the Judaism religion. The search is on for the descendants of the ancient priests and the implements and vestments of temple worship are being recreated. In fact, 32 temple articles have already been manufactured and are ready for the temple service (this is also setting the stage for the Anti-Christ to claim himself god as he has an idol image of himself placed in the temple during the mid-tribulation.)*[22]

Daniel 9:27b (NLB) says, "But after half this time (or the mid-tribulation) he (the Anti-Christ) will put an end to the sacrifices and offerings. Then as a climax to all his terrible deeds, he will set up a sacrilegious object that causes desolation."

A Good News Representative of the "The Good News" magazine had an interview with Leen Ritmeyer PhD, an archaeological architect, lecturer and teacher. He is perhaps the world's foremost authority on the architecture and archaeology of Jerusalem's Temple Mount site of the temple built by Solomon, Zerubbabel and the extensive renovation of the second temple by Herod the Great. Part of their conversation concerning the third Temple Mount went as follows:

---

21. Bates, Leon, A Tribulation Map, Texas: Bible Believer's Evangelistic Association, copyright, 1974.
22. Van Impe, Jack Dr., How A New Jewish Temple,'a correspondent to partners, Michigan: written by Jack Van Impe Ministries International, date is unknown.

GN: How do religiously observant Jews view the Temple Mount?

LR: For most religious Jews, that is the only site where they can worship God according to the Mosaic laws. Most Israelis don't care much about the Temple Mount. The thought of having animal sacrifices is repulsive to them. There is a large group of Jews who know they can't really worship God according to the Mosaic precepts unless they have a temple.*[23]

Two institutions, the "Temple Mount Faithful" and the "Temple Institute" are desperately trying to worship on the Temple Mount. The Jews within these institutions have been making the priestly garments, all gold and silver vessels, the silver trumpets and the golden lamp stand. They are ready to worship even tomorrow. However, of course, they need to start by building an altar. Under the present circumstances, they won't be allowed to build an altar or any other structure. Ultimately, they want to build a temple as well. The thing that is causing the difficulty is the Dome of the Rock still remains on the place where the Jewish temple stood in the past. They now want to start to build at least an altar and start sacrificing so that the Messiah will come and help them build their temple. A few years ago, the religious Jews had a Passover sacrifice on Mount Zion, so these people are desperate to start worshiping God according to their understanding.

GN: So they could start sacrifices without a temple if they only had an altar?

LR: Yes, that is true. The altar always goes before the temple. Noah built an altar. Abraham built an altar and David built an altar. The temple was built afterwards. The temple was built as a house for the Ark of the Covenant. They do not have the real Ark of the Covenant now, but through sacrifice they believe they do have a relationship with God.

GN: Do their conclusions about the location of the temple match your conclusions and research on the subject?

---

23. Council of Elders, Jerusalem's Temple Mount: Center Of Conflict Today , an article taken from the Good News Magazine, Ohio: Church Of God In Christ Publishers, Sept./Oct. Vol.9 No.5 issue, pgs. 8 & 9

LR: Yes, I've researched the location of the temple over many years and I believe I've been able to show that the foundation trenches of the walls of the Holy of Holies of Solomon's Temple can still be seen on the rock inside the Dome of the Rock. The Jewish community and other archaeologists believe that the temple of Solomon stood where the Dome of the Rock is now and they won't build a temple anywhere else.*[24]

3. The third sign setting the stage for the Great Tribulation is that all over the world, a cashless society using the number system has been put into effect. The use of a debit or credit card has all the information entailed in the card about the cardholder and can be used to buy anything by simply swiping the card in a small detector and punching in the pin number of the buyer's bank account and the money to pay for the item is withdrawn directly from the buyer's bank account without the option of actually using cash money. Code numbers are used to determine the price of merchandise today. The micro chips are now being invented. They are embedded under the skin of animals to determine their location if they are ever lost somewhere.

During the mid-tribulation, the false prophet will require every person to be sealed on their foreheads or on their hand the mark of the beast (the Anti-Christ) of 666. The figure will then become important in matters of buying and selling (or for world trade).

Harold L. Willmington, a teacher and writer of Eschatology, asked, "What does this mean? It seems to suggest that at the beginning of the tribulation, the world will adopt some sort of letter numbering system."*[25] This is also happening before our eyes today. When we apply for a job or file taxes or use as an ID number, the Social Security number is used.

Jack Van Impe says, "The Anti-Christ undoubtedly will use a computer to enslave the earth's population during the Great Tribulation hour. He will affect and maintain this control through commerce - the buying and selling of products. In order to make his plan operable, the

---

24.   Ibid. Pg. 10.
25.   Willmington, H.L., Signs Of The Times, Illinois: Tyndale House Publishers, Inc., third copyright, 1983, pgs. 152 & 153.

Anti-Christ will also introduce an international identification system in the form of a mark (possibly a laser tattoo) of 666 placed in the right hand or on the forehead of every individual participant. Without this mark, no man will be permitted to purchase or sell even the smallest item of merchandise."*[26] If anyone does not take the mark of the Anti-Christ, the threat of death is upon the individual's life.

During the mid-tribulation, there will be many tribulation saints who will resist the mark of the beast. They are warned not to take the mark of the beast or else they will suffer the wrath of God in the lake of fire. They much rather sacrifice their lives for Christ than to submit their lives to the devil incarnated in the body of the Anti-Christ.

Just think what the Anti-Christ can do with the micro-chip. He can use it to locate any person on earth if anyone runs or hides from his government or resist the mark; that person can be caught and be put to death. This would definitely happen to a tribulation saint who is bold to remain steadfast in the Christian faith. He knows his or her reward would be in heaven.

THE THREE CATEGORIES OF effect SEVEN JUDGMENTS DURING THE GREAT TRIBULATION

Suppose you were left behind after the Rapture and you are living during the Great Tribulation. You refuse to repent and accept Christ as your personal Savior to be a tribulation saint. You've accepted the mark of the beast of the Anti-Christ in order to buy or sell anything to survive. You are a candidate of experiencing God's wrath upon the wicked who have accepted the mark of the beast. God's wrath will be expressed in three categories of seven judgment activities. The first category is called the "Seven Seals", the second category is called the "Seven Trumpets" and the third category is called the, "Seven Bowls or Vials". The last category is God's intense wrath upon the wicked.

---

26. Van Impe, Jack, Bible Commentary Of Revelation, scripture, Revelation 13:16-18,
     Michigan: Printed in U.S.A., the year is unknown, pgs. 101 & 102.

The three categories of seven judgment activities are as follows:

THE SEVEN SEAL JUDGMENTS

- Anti-Christ dictatorship gov't (symbolized by the white horse)
- Peace taken away (symbolized by a red horse), global war, a lot of bloodshed (Rev.6:4) includes Ezekiel 38 war between Russia and its Arab allies against Israel as well as wars fought by the Anti-Christ.
- Famine intensifying economic inflation (symbolized by the black horse) (Rev. 6:5-6) due to global wars and droughts, etc.
- One fourth of world population will die because of war, hunger and diseases intensifies (symbolized by the pale horse) (Rev. 6:8).
- Tribulation saints will be slain for their faith in Christ (Rev. 6:9-11). The unsaved people will witness seeing this happen to the tribulation saints during the mid-tribulation.
- Earthquakes will increase in diverse places unexpectedly; the sun will lose part of its light and stars will fall. Mountain and islands will be moved because of earthquakes, (Rev. 6:12-14)
- Panic and terror of kings, commanders and wicked men will be universal (Rev. 6:15-19).

THE SEVEN TRUMPET JUDGMENTS

- Hail and fire falls mingled with blood; one third of trees and grass on earth will be burned up (Rev. 8:7)
- One third of fish in the sea, ships and crew will be destroyed by a large burning mountain (or a large asteroid) that will fall into the sea leaving one third of the seas full of blood of the fish and seamen (Rev. 8:8-9).
- Many will die from bitter poisoned rivers and spring waters by a burning great star from heaven. The name of the star is called "Wormwood". One third of the waters will be poisoned by this star or meteorite (Rev. 8:10-11).
- The sun is smitten giving off very little light and heat, one third of the stars and the light of the moon will be dim. The lack of heat and light will affect the temperature. Daylight will hardly shine (Rev. 8:12).
- Demonic creatures will torture the unsaved people for 5

months. They will wish to die, even try to die, but won't be able to; they will only continue to suffer (Rev. 9:1-11).

- Another one third of the world population will die by the armies of the Far East that will pass through by way of the Euphrates river route that will dry up. They will come with their dangerous weaponry (Rev. 9:13-18). They will march to fight against the Jewish nation and against the Anti-Christ who rules from Jerusalem due to his control of the world economy using his name and number sign 666,(Dan.11:44).
- More great earthquakes and great hail will occur (Rev. 11:19).

THE SEVEN BOWL OR VIAL JUDGMENTS

- Loathsome sores and boils will come upon the men and women who had the mark of the beast of 666 and who will worship his image (in the temple) (Rev. 16:2).
- Every sea becomes full of blood of dead sea animals (Rev. 16:3).
- All the rivers and spring waters will be totally bloody so that unsaved people will have to drink bloody water to quench their thirst (Rev. 16:4,5).
- All of a sudden the sun will give off fire and great heat that men will be scorched. Though the unsaved people will complain, they still will not repent. They will hate God for their torture (Rev. 16:8-9).
- Men will bite their tongues due to pain and of boil sores and still will not repent (Rev. 16:10-11).
- Preparation for the Battle of Armageddon when the angels of God will dry up the Euphrates river as a path for the kings and their armies from the east will do battle with the Jewish nation, Israel (Rev. 16:12-16). On their way to Israel, the armies of the east will kill one third of the population that are in their way. This would be the manifestation of the Trumpet judgment activity number 6. They will march towards Israel to fight against the Anti-Christ in Jerusalem and his armies because of his control over the world economy by his use of his mark 666 as well as fight Israel for her

oil goods at the Battle of Armageddon. The armies coming from the east to do battle against the Anti-Christ troubles him as he meets them to do battle prophesied in Daniel 11:44.

- A mighty earthquake will happen worse than any other earthquake that happens on earth, so that the cities of nations will fall. Even islands will flee away and mountains will be no more. Huge hailstones about 100lbs each will fall (Rev. 16:18-21). This occurs after the two witnesses are raptured (Rev. 11:12,13) which occurs after they minister in the second half of the Tribulation.

EVENTS FOLLOWING THE JUDGMENTS

Following the judgments, the second coming of Jesus Christ with His saints after the marriage feast in heaven (the Bride or the body of saints will have with the Bridegroom, Jesus Christ), will occur. The Jews are a downtrodden people. Their only hope is the return of the Lord, Jesus Christ. In the Old Testament Bible, it's predicted that at the end of the Great Tribulation, some unsaved nations will come against Israel. Then Jesus and the saints will rescue them and do battle against those nations (include the armies of the Anti-Christ, the armies from the Far East, and most unsaved nations who mistreat the Jews), Zechariah 14:1-4. These evil nations of people will be consumed by the fire of Jesus' and the saints' presence and by the word or sword of His mouth. The enemies' blood will be left on the land of Megiddo which is the valley between Mt. Carmel and the city of Jezreel. Armageddon is the Greek word for this area used for ancient battles. Thus, Megiddo became a symbol of the final conflict between God and the forces of evil. The blood of the enemies at the battle of Armageddon will extend for about 200 miles and that the blood shall be up to the horses' bridles, Rev.14:19-20. The prophet Isaiah in Isaiah 34:1-8 prophesied that the land shall be "soaked with blood". In Rev. 19:17-18, John prophesied and said that the flesh of every man (towards the end of the Great Tribulation) will be left for the buzzards, vultures and eagles to feast on.

The spirit of the Anti-Christ and the false prophet will be cast into the lake of fire, Rev. 19:20. Afterwards, Satan will be cast into the bottomless pit and remain in it for a thousand years so that Jesus can start His Millennial reign on the earth to initiate permanent world peace. What will happen during the Millennial Age will be discussed in Chapter 6. Just before Jesus' Millennial reign, He will judge and separate those nations who treated His Jewish brothers with kindness (called the sheep nations) from those nations who mistreated the Jews in Israel (called the goat nations) around the world that did not take part in the Battle of Armageddon. They shall be destroyed while the sheep nations will enter into the Millennial Age, Matthew 25:31-46.

After the Millennial Age, Satan will be released for awhile. God will test the nations to see which ones will remain faithful to the reign of Jesus Christ. Those who reject Christ's righteousness and fair authority will be destroyed and cast into hell. All the unsaved people from the beginning of the Gentile rule of Israel, who died in their sins, will be raised at the second resurrection to face the White Throne Judgment of Christ. If their names are not found in the Lord's Book of Life, they will be cast into the Lake of Fire along with Satan and his demons, Rev. 20:11-15.

If you are not saved in Christ, do you desire to go through the tortures of God's wrath during the Great Tribulation period if you missed the Rapture? You may say I do not believe that a Rapture will occur nor the Great Tribulation. My friend, whether you are a believer or a non-believer, the things that the Bible says will happen in our day and age have and will happen. God is not a God that He should lie nor a man that He should repent. The events happening today are already setting the stage for the rapture to happen and for the Great Tribulation to manifest in the near future.

HOW TO AVOID THE GREAT TRIBULATION

Again, If you are not saved in Christ, do you want to go through the tortures of God's wrath during the Great Tribulation period if you are alive? If you die in your sins without Christ, do you want your eternal spirit to live forever in hell's fire? Since the Rapture has not occurred yet, you still have time to be saved and avoid the terrible suffering and death both in hell and in the Great Tribulation that will last for seven years.

Admit that you are an imperfect sinner, repent of your sins in that you have not lived up to God's standard written in the Bible and ask Jesus Christ into your heart, because Jesus was the only one who willfully died and shed His blood on the cross for your sins and for sins of the whole human race. Ask Jesus to be Lord of your life by faith, because you ask with the belief that Christ is alive today to save you. The moment you call upon the name of Jesus into your life, Jesus' Spirit called the Holy Spirit immediately enters your dormant human spirit to enliven you with the eternal Spirit of God. You'll automatically be a part of God's family and kingdom and not Satan's kingdom. You'll be a new creature in Christ, a child of God. Even as a child of God, you will still make mistakes. This will happen, because you need to know God's way of living and doing things.

If you miss it in life, just repent of your wrong doing and God will cleanse away all unrighteousness. God immediately forgives you each time you mess up. As you grow in the knowledge of God's word by a minister in a church or at a Bible Study and grow by the Holy Spirit within you, you won't want to practice sin or do the bad habits you use to do. With your cooperation and by the unction of the Holy Spirit within you as a Christian, Jesus' Spirit lives in you to give you the strength to overcome trials and persecutions in life. He'll help you to live the Christian life. You cannot live it in your own spiritual strength. He is the Spirit of joy, peace, love, patience, long suffering, goodness, kindness and temperance living and growing in you.

God so loved you that he gave His Son, Jesus that if you believe and accept Him, you will not perish, but have everlasting life on earth and in heaven. You will be counted worthy to be in the Rapture, because you will have Jesus' Spirit - the Holy Spirit. The Holy Spirit of God and the angels determine your exit out of the earth and draw you and other true Christians to Christ at the Rapture. It is not God's will that any should perish. He says in His word, choose you this day life in Christ or death in Satan. The God of love wishes for you to choose life in His Son, Jesus.

It is hoped that chapter five didn't frighten the reader, but alerted and warned the reader, if unsaved, how important it is to abide in God's mercy through the acceptance of His Son, Jesus Christ. If you are not a Christian, won't you consider being one? God does not want you to miss the Rapture and be left behind to face the seven year period of the Great Tribulation, nor face the White Throne Judgment of Christ if one dies in his or her sins without Christ's Spirit. This would be considered the Second Resurrection of the unsaved dead.

During the Great Tribulation period, it will be difficult to be and stay a Christian. However, with the help of the Holy Spirit, He will give the Tribulation saints encouragement by the word they will hear from the evangelists in the Tribulation period to be obedient to God's statutes by their own effort and responsibility of not taking the mark of the Anti-Christ; but persevere to keep the faith in Christ, Rev. 14: 9-13. The Holy Spirit will not reside within the Tribulation saints, but ministers to them the way He ministered to the Prophets in the Old Testament outwardly upon them and not inwardly the way the Holy Spirit ministers within the Church body as a guider, strengthener, teacher and helper to do God's will during the Church Age, John 14:15-17,Acts 2: 4. That is why It is important to accept Jesus Christ today. Now is the time to receive salvation while there is still time before the rapture occurs, 2Corinthians 6:2. You do not want to be left behind to live in the Great Tribulation period.

All true Christians (Christian Jews and gentiles) as well as the Jews who died in Abraham's bosom who accepted what Jesus did on the cross to set them free to live in heaven with Him, will be in the First Resurrection which will also include the tribulation saints who give their lives to Christ during the seven year period of the Great Tribulation, and the sheep nations who treat Israeli people with kindness during the Great Tribulation period when Christ judges the nations just before He begins His Millennial Reign on earth. This will be discussed further in Chapter six.

CHAPTER 6

THE MILLENNIAL AGE

Before the Millennial Age and before the Battle of Armageddon when Jesus Christ's Spirit and the angels of heaven are sent forth to gather the nations, the nations or a group of nations of people will be judged and divided as sheep separated from the goats. They will be judged based on how they treat the brethren of Jesus Christ who are the people of Israel. The sheep nations who remain on earth and weren't involved in the Battle of Armageddon, will enter into the blessings of the Millennial Age. The goat nations will be destroyed during the Battle of Armageddon. After the Great White Throne Judgment, the souls of the goat nations who worshiped the beast, the Anti-Christ and accepted the mark of the beast, 666, will be sent to everlasting torment in the lake of fire, Rev. 20:11-15.

The 'Millennium' is defined as the thousand year period when Jesus Christ comes back the second time to rule and reign with His saints over the earth, Rev. 19:11-16; 20:1-9.*[27] Christ will rule the earth with a rod of Iron or with firm authority and with love.

Rev. 2:27 (as well as Ps 2:9) says, "He (Jesus) shall rule them with a rod of iron. They shall be dashed to pieces like the potter's vessels;" that is, Jesus' authority will crush the nations that resist Him or are rebellious.

Another synonym for millennium is "the Dispensation Pre-Millennialism. This is the belief that Jesus will come back to earth after a

---

27. Ibid. Nelson's Illustrative Bible Dictionary, pg. 709 column 1.

seven year tribulation and will rule during a 1000 year millennium of peace on earth. Most dispensational pre-millennialists are pre-tribulationists; they understand Rev. 4:1-2, which refers to the rapture of the Church.*[28]

What do dispensational pre-millennialists emphasize? They believe the rapture and the second coming of Jesus are two separate events. The rapture comes before the Great Tribulation and the second coming of Christ occurs after it.

According to the dispensational pre-millennialists: a.) During the Great Tribulation many Jews will turn to Jesus Christ. b.) The Jews will still receive the land described in Gen. 15:18 from the river of Egypt to the great river Euphrates. Scriptures that support the belief of the dispensational pre-millennialists: a.) God will remove Christians before the outpouring of God's Wrath during the Great Tribulation, 1Thess. 5:9, Rev. 3:10. Prominent dispensational pre-millennialists include: J. Nelson Darby, C.I. Scofield, Hal Lindsey, Charles Stanley and Tim Lahaye.*[29]

Several things must take place during the Millennial Age:

Satan will be bound for 1000 years in the bottomless pit. Angels from heaven will place him there. In Rev. 20:1-3 (NKJV) John, the apostle says, "Then I saw an angel coming down from heaven, having the key to the bottomless pit and a great chain in his hand."

Vs. 2, " He laid hold of the Dragon, that serpent of old, who is the Devil and Satan and bound him for a thousand years."

Vs. 3, "And he cast him into the bottomless pit and shut him up and set a seal on him so that he should deceive the nations no more till the 1000 years were finished. But after these things, he must be released for a little while."

A Theocratic government will be established by Jesus Christ at His second coming. This form of government will promote world-wide peace, love and justice. Fear will have no place within the human race, nor will people fear the wild animals. Even a child will sit with a lion without the lion hurting the child, Isaiah 11:3-9. Jesus' place of ruler-ship will take

---

28. Jones, Timothy Paul, Four Views Of The End Times, a 14 panel pamphlet, California: Rose Publishing Co., copyright, 2006.
29. Ibid. Pre-Millennialism Section. 39

place in the City of Jerusalem or in the City of David. In Jeremiah 3:17 (NKJV), it says, "At that time (the day of the Lord) Jerusalem shall be called the Throne of the Lord and all the nations shall be gathered to it in the name of the Lord, to Jerusalem. No more shall they (the sheep nations) follow the dictates of their evil hearts."

Human life will be prolonged. Psalms 92:13-14 (NKJV) says, "Those who are planted in the house of the Lord shall flourish in the courts of our God. They shall bear fruit in old age. They shall be fresh and flourishing …" Most of the Gentile nations will still have the sin nature, however, it will not be activated in relation to other Gentiles, because Satan will be bound in the bottomless pit for 1000 years. The human race will increase. Marriages between men and women will still continue and their bodies will still be of the Adamic nature.

The sun and the moon will be brighter, because more of their reflection comes from the glory of Christ's Presence. Isaiah 30:26 (NKJV) says, " Moreover, the light of the moon will be as the light of the sun, and the light of the sun will be sevenfold as the light of seven days in the day that the Lord binds up the bruise of His people and heals the stroke of their wound."

The tribulation saints will serve God in His temple. Jesus will be the High Priest. He is the High Priest in heaven right now ever making intercession for His people. Animal sacrifices and the celebration of the Passover and the Feast of Tabernacles the Jews restore during the first 3 1/2 years of the great tribulation, will not be necessary; because Jesus Christ fulfilled the representation of the Passover, animal sacrifices and the Feast of Tabernacles, Rev. 7:14-17.

According to the article in the Good News Magazine entitled, "The Biblical Festivals That Show How God Will Bring World Peace," by Roger Foster, under the subtitle, "A Millennium Of Global Restoration," Mr. Foster said that the Feast of Tabernacles or the Festival of Ingathering, represents the first 1000 years of the restorative rule of Jesus Christ on earth. During the first part of His rule, He will use several techniques to convince a deceived world that He really is the divine Son of God with the power to give or refuse blessings: a.) He will establish Jerusalem as the capital of His Kingdom, Zech. 14:1-9; b)

He will judge between many peoples and will settle disputes for strong nations far and wide. They will beat their swords into plowshares and their spears into pruning hooks. A nation will not take up a sword against a nation, nor will they train for war anymore, Micah 4:2-3 (NIV); c.) "And it shall be that whichever of the families of the earth do not come up to Jerusalem to worship the King, the Lord of Hosts, on them there will be no rain, "Zech.14:16-19. Isaiah 9: 7 (NIV) says, "Christ's righteous rule will soon secure a peace the world has never known before. Of the increase of His government and peace, there will be no end upon the throne of David and over His Kingdom to order it, establish it with judgment and justice from that time forward; even forevermore. The zeal of the Lord of Host will perform this."*30

The Jewish nation ruled by King David and the Bride of Christ will be assigned to be the head and ruler over the Gentile nations, and Jews with Jesus Christ. Deut. 28:13 and Rev.5:10.

After the Millennial Age, Satan will be loosed to resume his deceit to the nations. This will be a time of testing upon the Gentile nations to see if the Gentiles will maintain their faithfulness to Christ and abide by His government. Apostasy takes place. Even other nations will encamp around the righteous who abide in and with Christ. These other Gentiles that increased during the Millennial age come in the spirit of Gog and Magog. They will come against Jerusalem again. These gentile nations do not seem to learn that they can never win a war against God and His people. When will they ever learn? However, God rains down fire and brimstone upon the enemy and saves the righteous Gentiles. Satan is cast into the lake of fire to live in it forever, Rev. 20:7-10.

The White Throne Judgment: After the second resurrection of the wicked dead they will be judged by their wicked deeds. Whoever does not have his or her name written in the Book of Life will be cast into the Lake of Fire for his or her soul to be tormented forever, Rev. 20:11-15.

---

30 Ibid. Good News Magazine, pg. 26.

PRE MILLENNIALISM VS. AMILLENNIALISM AND POST MILLENNIALISM

There are some theologians that have a different view concerning when the millennial reign of Christ will take place on earth. The author will discuss other theologians' different beliefs of the millennium and its occurrence. Then the author will compare the Christian beliefs of the dispensational pre-millennialism with the beliefs of the amillennialism and the post-millennialism. First, amillennialism and post-millennialism will be defined; then beliefs will be listed and a list of theologians who believe and teach on their concept.

The author will counteract some of the Amillennialists' and Post-millennialists' beliefs in the form of a chart: What is Amillennialism? Amillennialism is the belief that Jesus will come again someday. There is no literal 1000 year rule by Jesus on the earth, rather, the millennium symbolizes Christ's reign in the lives of His people from the beginning of the Church Age until His second coming. It is believed that Christ triumphed over Satan through His death and resurrection in 30 A.D. and restrained the power of Satan on the earth, Rev. 20:1-3.

The persecution of Tribulation Saints will occur until Jesus comes again as will the expansion of God's Kingdom (the millennium). The author would like to inject the error of this belief in that the Tribulation afflicting the believers before the rapture are considered birth pangs or the beginning of sorrows, Matt. 24:8. However, they are setting the stage for the same sorrows to intensify during the Great Tribulation after the rapture. The afflicting tribulation before the rapture is not the same as the Great Tribulation that the tribulation saints will experience after the rapture. The Amillennialist does not make this distinction.

Another belief of the Amillennialist is that when Christ returns, He will immediately defeat the power of evil, resurrect the saved and the unsaved, and judge and deliver them to their eternal destinies.

According to the Amillennialists:

1. The Great Tribulation represents disasters, wars and persecutions that have occurred throughout church history.

2. The first resurrection could refer to the spiritual resurrection, Rev. 20:4.

3. The second coming of Christ and the resurrection of the saved and the unsaved will occur at the same time, Daniel 12:2-3, John 5:28-29. The author injects that these two scriptures are misinterpreted by the Amillennialists. They do not make the distinction that when the saved are awakened to everlasting life, it is considered the first resurrection. The ones who are awakened to shame and everlasting contempt are considered to be in the second resurrection. There is a 1000 year difference between the first and second resurrections. Therefore, the saved and unsaved are not resurrected at the same time.

4. The saints are on earth during the tribulation, Rev. 13:7. The author injects that this scripture is misinterpreted. This scripture is talking about the tribulation saints not the redeemed church body that had been raptured. The Anti-Christ will make war and overcome the tribulation saints. Again, the Amillennialist fails to distinguish between the saints of the body of Christ that are raptured from the tribulation saints whom the Anti-Christ makes war against during the mid-tribulation.

When has Amillennialism been popular? Amillennialism became popular in the fifth century mainly promoted by St. Augustine. Amillennialism has remained widespread throughout church history.

Who are the Amillennialists? Some of the Protestant reformers, such as Martin Luther, John Calvin and the Evangelical theologians such as, Abraham Kuyper, Herschel Hobbs, Stanley Grenz and E.Y. Mullins.

The chart of argument and resolution between the Amillennialists and Pre-Millennialists.*[31]:

Amillennialist's Belief	Dispensational Pre-Millennialist's Belief
The Second Coming of Jesus Christ can happen at any time.	The Second Coming of Christ comes at the end of the 7 year Great Tribulation, Rev. 19:11-16..
There is no literal Millennium. It symbolizes that the Millennium reigns in the hearts of believers and that Satan's power is restrained on earth.	The Millennial Age is a literal event following the Battle of Armageddon, Rev. 20:1-3. Satan is bound 1000 years. True, Christ reigns in the hearts of saints, however, Christ's Kingdom is demonstrated outwardly on earth for 1000 years. Kingdom of Christ starts in Jerusalem, Jeremiah 3:17.
Christians will live and be persecuted in the Great Tribulation until Jesus Christ's second coming.	The redeemed church of Christ will be raptured and not encounter the Wrath of God, 1Thess. 5:9. During the mid-tribulation, the tribulation saints (left behind after the rapture, not the redeemed church body), will be drastically persecuted and slaughtered by the Anti-Christ, Rev.19:17.
The rapture of the saved and the unsaved will happen at the same time.	No, the rapture of the saved redeemed church occurs before the unsaved are resurrected to face judgment. 1Thess. 4:13-18. This scripture does not indicate the unsaved are raptured at the same time with the saved. The unsaved are raised to face the White Throne Judgment Seat of Christ, Rev. 20:11-15.

---

31.   Ibid. Four Views Of The End Times, the Amillennialism section.

Amillennialist's Belief	Dispensational Pre-Millennialist's Belief
The Great Tribulation represents wars, disasters and persecution that have occurred throughout church history.	Jesus said in Matt 24:8 that the war earthquakes and persecutions were birth pangs or the beginning of sorrows; the end is not yet. During the mid-tribulation, wars, earthquakes and disasters will greatly intensify. The body of Christ, (the church), does not encounter this, because they are already in heaven, so that church history does not extend into the Great Tribulation. Only the tribulation saints (not the church body that was raptured) will have to suffer persecution because of their stand for Jesus Christ by the Anti-Christ. The raptured Church will not encounter the Anti-Christ. He can't manifest unless the body of Christ is raptured, 2 Thess. 2:7-8.
The first resurrection symbolizes the spiritual resurrection of persons who put their trust in Christ (or the new birth experience).	The spiritual resurrection is an inward experience of a believer's spirit being redeemed by the Holy Spirit. This is not symbolized in the first resurrection. This salvation experience qualifies the believer to be in the first resurrection at the rapture. Towards the end of the Great Tribulation, the tribulation saints will be in the first resurrection when they are raptured.

What is Post-Millennialism? Post-Millennialism is the belief that the second coming of Christ will occur after the Millennium. It is believed that the Post-Millennialists place great confidence in the preaching of the gospel. They contend that the gospel will eventually spread in such a way that nearly everyone in the world will turn to Jesus Christ.

This teaches that through the contemporary Charismatic movement, God has been binding Satan. When the church recognizes the fullness of its power through the Holy Spirit, the church will establish God's Kingdom on earth and usher in the Millennium or the golden age. The Post-Millennialists believe that this golden age is described in such scripture as Psalms 2:8, Isaiah 2:2-4, Jeremiah 31:34, Daniel 2:35 and Micah 4:1-4. Post-Millennialists tend to transform societies and individual lives.*[32]

According to Post-Millennialists:

During the Millennium, Christ will rule the earth through His Spirit and through the church. Christ will not, however, be physically present on earth.

Like the belief of the Amillennialists, the Post-Millennialists believe that the resurrection depicted in Rev. 20:4, represents the spiritual regeneration of people who trust Jesus Christ.

The second coming of Christ, the final conflict between good and evil, the defeat of Satan, the physical resurrection of a people, and the final judgment, will occur together immediately after the Millennium.

When Has Post-Millennialism been popular? The earliest writer who was clearly Post-Millennialist was Joachim of Fiore (1135-1202), although many historians believe that earlier church leaders, such as, Eusebius of Caesarea, Athanasuis of Alexandrea and Augustine of Hippo were also Post-Millennialists.

During the 1800s, Post-Millennialism increased in popularity. Some Christians even believed that the increased work of missionaries throughout the world represented the beginning of the Millennium. During the early 1900s, a world war and an economic depression raise questions in many people's minds about whether the world was actually becoming a better place. As a result, the Post-Millennialism diminished in popularity.

Prominent Post-Millennialists include: famous preachers; such as, Jonathan Edwards, Charles Haddon Spurgeon and theologians such as B.B. Warfield, Augustus Strong, Charles Hodge, R.L. Dabney, Loraine Boettner and R.C. Sproul.*[33]

---

32. Ibid. Post-Millennialism section.
33. Ibid.

The Chart of argument and resolution between Post-Millennialism and Pre-Millennialsm:

Post-Millennialists' Belief	Dispensational Pre-Millennialists' Belief
The rapture and the second coming of Christ occur at the same time for both the save and the unsaved.	No, the rapture and the second coming of Christ do not occur at the same time. Both events are separated by the 7 year Great Tribulation period. In the rapture, Jesus is coming suspended in the air to meet the redeemed body of Christ in secret. At the time of the Battle of Armageddon, Jesus touches the earth on a white horse along with His church body and the tribulation saints. This would be His second coming, Rev. 19:11-16.
Jesus will return after the Millennial Age	Rev. 19:11-21 distinctly says that Jesus will come on a white horse to earth with the armies of heaven clothed in fine linen, white and clean. They will war against the Anti-Christ and his armies which include the false prophet. This war is called the Battle of Armageddon. This happens before Christ sets up His Millennial reign, not after. Christ sets up His Millennial reign after the Battle of Armageddon, Rev. 20:1-10.
The tribulation is the conflict between good and evil since Jesus' death	The tribulation activities stated in Matt. 24:3-12, (Jesus said) were birth pangs or the beginning of sorrows. This kind of tribulation is setting the stage for the tribulation that will intensify greatly during the Great Tribulation Period. Tribulation does not stop at Jesus' resurrection. It continues for as long as man lives on earth. There will be no world peace until Jesus comes to the earth to set up His Millennial reign.

Post-millenniarism' Belief	Dispensational Pre-Millennialists' Belief
The Christians,(the body of Christ), will continue to share the gospel and because of this, they will suffer even during the Great Tribulation.	The Post-Millennialists make no distinction between the body of Christ who shares the gospel before they're raptured, and the Tribulation saints in the Great Tribulation who were left behind after the rapture. The Tribulation saints and the 144,000 Jews will be the evangelists from the beginning through the mid-tribulation. Then they will be raptured, the 144,000 Jews during the mid-tribulation in Rev. 14:1-5 and the tribulation saints towards the end of the mid-tribulation before the vial judgment activities, Rev. 15:1-5.
There will be no literal Millennial Age. The Millennial refers to a period of peace when the gospel reaches all people.	Not true, there will be a literal Millennial Age after Jesus Christ and His saints come back to earth to win in the Battle of Armageddon, Rev. 19:11-20:5. Not everyone on earth is going to accept the gospel of God. Therefore, there can never be peace on earth, once again, until Jesus sets up His Millennial reign.

The author concludes that by comparing the beliefs of the Pre-Millennialists with the beliefs of the Amillennialists and the Post-Millennialists, you can acknowledge that the beliefs of the Pre-Millennialists are in accord with the scriptures in the word of God, the Holy Bible with the correct interpretation. The Amillenialists and the Post-Millennialists try to make the scriptures comply with how they think, instead of reading the text or scripture in its context to draw out the true meaning of what the scripture means; especially, concerning the occurrence of the Millennial Age, the rapture and making a distinction between the body of Christ and the tribulation saints. There is no scripture that states that the body of Christ will go through the Great Tribulation. Only the tribulation saints will experience the dictatorship of the Anti-Christ during the Great Tribulation seven year period.

The Amillennialists and the Post-Millennialists make no distinction between the tribulations called birth pangs mentioned in Matt. chapter 24:3-12, and the tribulations that are poured out by the wrath of God upon the wicked people during the Great Tribulation period. They tie in the tribulations of today with the tribulations that will occur intensely during the Great Tribulation period. The difference is that the tribulations during the Great Tribulation are more intense or more severe for those who are left behind after the rapture, because they are living a wicked life and taking on the mark of the Anti-Christ, 666. The church body of Christ is now on earth experiencing the tribulation birth pangs. Jesus said, those who endure shall be saved (in the rapture), Matt. 24:13. According to 1Thess. 5:9, the body of Christ will not experience the wrath of God, which will be exhibited during the Great Tribulation; therefore the body of Christ will be raptured. The Amillennialists and the Post-Millennialists do not believe in a pre-tribulation rapture. This is why they believe the Church Age extends into the Great Tribulation period and that the rapture will occur at the same time of Jesus' second coming. This is not biblically correct and is erroneous.

CHAPTER 7

THE PERFECT AGE OR THE DISPENSATION OF THE FULLNESS OF TIME OR AGE OF ETERNITY

Several things will occur during the Perfect Age or during the Dispensation of The Fullness of Time or the Age of Eternity:

1. After the Great White Throne Judgment, God begins to renovate the earth with fire, 2Peter 3:10-13 and Rev. 21:1-4. The exterior surface shall be changed. All that sin brought into existence, such as, thorns, thistles, diseases, insect pests, etc., shall be destroyed. Animals and vegetation will be destroyed. The atmosphere will be purified, forever free from evil spirits.*[34] While this is occurring, the saints and righteous Gentiles are protected in the heavenly New City of Jerusalem.

2. The earth is restored like the Garden of Eden. Health is maintained by the use of the leaves on the Tree of Life. The River of Life's source of health and youth comes from the Throne of God.

3. A New City called The New Jerusalem, which the Bride of Christ inhabits, comes down out of Heaven and settles on the New Earth. The City is 1500 miles long and 1500 miles wide. The wall is 144 cubit feet thick and high or 216 ft thick and high. The City extends like the distance between Florida and Maine. The walls have 3 gates on each side of the wall made of one large pearl. The City streets are made of gold. The foundation of the City wall is made of various colored gems. The gates are named after the 12 tribes of Israel. In the center of the City is the River of Life lined with the Tree of Life which encompasses a cluster

---

34. Ibid. Dispensational Truth, pg. 145, column 2.

of trees each bearing fruit for the healing of the nations, Rev. 21:9-22:5.*35

4. There will be no more tears, sorrow nor pain, Rev.21:2-8.

5. There will be worship and praise in the City Temple which is God's Presence in the midst of His people. There will not be a physical temple, Rev. 21:3-4.

6. The City had no need of the sun or of the moon to shine in it, for the glory of God illuminated it. The Lamb is the light. The nations of those who are saved shall walk in its light and the kings of the earth bring their glory and honor into it, Rev. 21:23-26.

CONCLUSION

The signs of the times and the teachings of the Book of Revelation are not to frighten anyone, but to alert and inform the believers, unbelievers and the backslidden saints to get their lives together in committing or recommitting their lives to God by accepting Jesus Christ in their hearts as their personal Savior. If not, they will be left behind when the rapture occurs and will end up facing the Wrath of God which is the Great Tribulation judgment period. Even if they are left behind, God's mercy is extended to them allowing them to hear the gospel that will be shared by the 144,000 Jews and giving them the opportunity to accept Jesus as their personal Savior from the beginning of the Tribulation to the mid-tribulation; however, again, it will be very difficult to maintain the Christian faith. If the tribulation saints refuse to take the mark of the Anti-Christ during the mid-tribulation, they will be either beheaded or killed by a weapon. That is why Jesus instructs in Rev. 2:10 for the tribulation saints to be faithful unto death and He will reward them with the crown of life.

The urgency of the closeness of the rapture, by knowing the signs of the times and being aware of what will happen in the future concerning the events of the Great Tribulation, will stir the spirit of every Christian

---

35. Ibid. Pg. 146, column 2.

believer to do the work of evangelism to get the unbelievers and the backslidden saints back into the Kingdom of God by sharing the gospel of Jesus Christ. Their proclamation of the gospel should include some signs that would convey the closeness of Jesus' coming and that the patience of God's grace for salvation is coming to an end at the time of the rapture.

According to Acts 3:19-21, God will not send Jesus to get His church body, unless the church body of Christians are restored, living in their spiritual potential with the fruit of the Spirit operating and doing the works that Jesus did. Jesus is not coming back for sick and weak Christians. It is the responsibility of the Holy Spirit to prepare the body of Christ by refining the character, restoring the vessels from sin and sickness and empowering the body of Christ to do the works that Jesus did; that is, sharing the gospel, casting out demons and healing the sick, as well as learning to practice the presence of the Holy Spirit or of God. Once the body of Christ obtains this level of spiritual maturity and exhibits this experience, this would be the beginning of revival of the fire of the Holy Spirit operating within the vessels of the church body of believers. This revival will then spread into the community as evangelism is taken into the streets by the spirit-filled believers.

How long will the revival in our nation and in other nations last? We do not know; however, this one thing the author knows, once your see the revival of the move of God's Spirit invade the atmosphere and invade with His glory within the vessels of believers, know the next event to happen is the rapture. It is closer than you think.

For those theologians and some Christians who believe that the rapture will happen during the mid-tribulation or the post-tribulation, are misinterpreting the scripture. In 1Thess. 5:9, it states that "it is not appointed to the church body of Christ to encounter the wrath of God; but to receive salvation spiritually and physically through our Lord, Christ Jesus."

They also misinterpret 2Thess. 2:7-8, which states in a short statement, "Only He (the Holy Spirit within the body of Christ) who retrains is taken out of the way (rapture), the lawless one (the Anti-Christ) will be revealed. The Lord Jesus will slay him with the breath of His mouth and bring him to an end by His appearing at His coming (second coming). This is proof to the Amillennialists and the Post-Millennialists that the rapture will occur before the Great Tribulation and that it is a pre-tribulation event.

The Amillennialists and the Post-Millennialists both believe that the Millennium is not literally the physical kingdom of Christ on earth. The Amillenialists believe the Millennium is already taking place in the hearts of all Christians. The Post-Millennialists believe the whole world will submit to the hearing and acceptance of the gospel of Christ and therefore, the Millennium will already exist on earth before the second coming of Christ.

This too is erroneous thinking. This belief does not agree with the interpretation of the scripture, Rev. 19:11-21 which indicates that Jesus and His armies of heaven will return to earth to fight and win in the Battle of Armageddon and then Jesus will literally set up His Millennial kingdom, Rev. 20:4-6 and Zech. 14:8-11.

The author hopes that whoever reads this Eschatology book will be blessed and eventually share the information with other believers, as well as unbelievers who are willing to hear the gospel of Jesus and His coming. It is also hoped that when unbelievers read this book, they will make a decision to accept Jesus into their lives, so that they will be counted worthy to be in the rapture.

BIBLIOGRAPHY

BOOK REFERENCE MATERIALS:

1. Dake Finis, Jennings, "Annotated Reference Bible." (KJV) Georgia: copyright, 1973 by F.J. Dake.

2. Guralnik, David, Chief Editor, "Webster's New World Dictionary." Ohio: William Collins Publishers, Inc., copyright, 1979.

3. Hurlbut, Jesse, L., "The Story Of The Christian Church." Michigan: Latest revised by Zondervan Publishing House, copyright, 1970.

4. Larkin, Clarence, "Dispensational Truth." Pennsylvania, U.S.A.: Rev. Clarence Larkin Est. Publishers, copyright, 1920.

5. Martin, Walter, "The Kingdom Of Cults." Minnesota: Published by Bethany House Publishers, revised copyright, 2003.

6. Nelson Thomas, "Nelson's Illustrated Bible Dictionary." General Ed., Herbert Lockyer, Sr., Tennessee: Thomas Nelson Publishers, 1986.

7. Nelson, Thomas, "The Nelson Study Bible." (NKJV) commentary, Tennessee: Thomas Nelson Publishers, revised 1982.

8. Strong, James, "The Exhaustive Concordance Of The Bible." (KJV) Nashville: Abingdon Pres, New Jersey: copyright by James Strong, 1890.

9. Sutton, Hilton, Th.D., "The Book Of Revelation Revealed." Texas: Hilton Sutton World Ministry Publishers, revised, 2007.

10. Van Impe, Jack, Dr., "Revelation Revealed Verse By Verse." A commentary from the Prophecy Bible, Michigan: Printed in the U.S.A. (year is unknown).

11. Willmington, H.L., "Signs Of The Times." Illinois: Tyndale House Publishers, Inc., third copyright, 1983.

MAGAZINES , NEWSLETTERS , PAMPHLETS & CHARTS :

12. Bates, Leon, "<u>A Tribulation Map</u>." Texas: Bible Believers' Evangelistic Association, 1974.

13. Bjornstad, James Dr. and Staff, "<u>Christianity, Cults and Religions</u>." A folded mini panel chart, California: Rose Publishing Co., copyright, 2005.

14. Council of Elders, "<u>Jerusalem's Temple Mount: Center Of Conflict Today</u>." An article taken from the Good News Magazine, Ohio: Church Of God In Christ Publishers, Sept./Oct., 2004 Vol.9 No.5 issue.

15. Eckstein, Yechiel Rabbi, Exec. Dir., "<u>The SHORESH</u>." A newsletter, Illinois: Published by The International Fellowship of Christian and Jews, Vol.8 No.8, August 2002 issue.

16. Goodman, Hirsh, Chief ed., "<u>The Jerusalem Report</u>." Israel: Jerusalem Report Publications Ltd., June 13, 1991 issue.

17. Jones, Timothy Paul, "<u>Four Views Of the End Times</u>." A 14 panel pamphlet, California: Rose Publishing co. copyright, 2006.

18. Van Impe, Jack Dr., "<u>How a New Jewish Temple in Jerusalem Is Tied To the Anti-Christ</u>." A correspondent to partners, Michigan: written by Jack Van Impe Ministries International (date is unknown).

VIDEO TAPE S CASSETTE TAPE S , DVD S AND COMPUTER RESEARCH:

19. Armstrong, Roger Min., "Post-Tribulation Rapture." A computer research information from www.westernfront.com under Hal Lindsey Ministries, California: At the End- Time Bible Prophecy Conference, 2007.

20. Blair, Charles Dr., "The March Of Prophecy." Part 2 and Part 3, video tapes, Colorado: produced by The Charles Blair Foundation, 2002.

21. Hagee, John, "Book Of Revelation." 8 CDs, Texas: Produced by the John Hagee Ministries, 2007.

22. Lindsey, Hal, "Vanished Into Thin Air." A video tape, California: Wester Front Ltd. Publishing (year is unknown).

23. Pastor of Christian Assembly Pentecostal Church in USA, "The Third World War," a leaflet, a computer research information from www.cai.org/leaflets/thethirdworldwar

24. Sutton, Hilton, "The Book Of Revelation.", 14 cassette tapes, Texas: Hilton Sutton World Ministries Publications, 2001.

25. Sutton, Hilton, "Russia And Her Allies Coming Against Israel And The Rapture." A monthly CD for the months of July and August, Texas: Hilton Sutton World Ministries Publications, 2007.

26. Wilson, Darren, "Finger Of God." A commentary collected on a DVD, California: Wanderlust Productions, 2006.